Build APIs You Won't

Everyone and their dog wants an API, so you should probably learn how to build them.

Phil Sturgeon

Build APIs You Won't Hate

Everyone and their dog wants an API, so you should probably learn how to build them.

Phil Sturgeon

This book is for sale at apisyouwonthate.com

This version was published on 2015-08-11

ISBN 978-0692232699

A huge thank you to all the developers and other folks who built the technologies this book talks about.

I would also like to thank everyone who bought an early copy of this book on LeanPub. 2014 was a really messed up year for me, and those book sales kept me going, and kept me motivated to finish the book on time.

Without you, I would be much further away from getting my boat.

Contents

Introduction

A lot of articles and tutorials talk about REST and with a varying level of accuracy. Some claim that certain things are more RESTful than others whilst actually having very little to do with REST. The word REST has been so utterly misused for the last seven or eight years that it actually means nothing anymore, and a large chunk of the API development community has moved to terms like Hypermedia API to represent what was intended by the original meaning of REST before it was utterly ruined. This book will not get too hung up on these politics. It will mostly outline the pros and cons of various approaches, only giving you the "one true way" when the other approaches are all patently awful (like SOAP and XML-RPC).

Whilst trying to learn about API development, I found most resources out there to be horribly lacking or specifically aimed at one single framework. Many tutorials and books use apples and pears examples that are not concrete enough, or talk like listing /users and /users/1 are the only endpoints you will ever need. Between 2012 and 2014, I worked for a company called Kapture where my primary function was to inherit, rebuild, maintain and further develop a fairly large API with many different endpoints exposing a lot of different use cases.

This book will discuss the theory of designing and building APIs in any language or framework. This theory will be applied in examples built mostly in PHP, with some Ruby and Python too. The book will not be too code-heavy regardless, since reading code is no fun.

By the end of this book, you will have built an API that can create, read, update, delete things, handle searching, and do everything else a good Hypermedia API needs to do.

Sample Code

This book covers both theory which is applicable to any language, and it covers concrete examples using source code written in PHP. PHP was selected mostly because it had to be written in something, but all content is applicable to any language.

The code can be downloaded in a few ways.

a) You can clone it:

```
1   $ git clone https://github.com/philsturgeon/build-apis-you-wont-hate.git
```

b) Browse around it:

> https://github.com/philsturgeon/build-apis-you-wont-hate

c) Download it as a `.zip` file:

> http://bit.ly/apisyouwonthate-zip

The book assumes a few things in relation to this same code.

1. You have PHP 5.4 available.
2. You are ok playing with Laravel 4, even if you have no experience with it.
3. You place the contents in `~/apisyouwonthate`.

If you put the sample code somewhere else, then update the path in the examples.

1. Useful Database Seeding

1.1 Introduction

The first step to creating any sort of application is creating the database. Whether you are using some sort of relational platform, MongoDB, Riak, or whatever, you will need a vague idea of how your data is going to be stored.

For relational databases it is very likely you will start off your planning with an entity-relationship diagram. For document based databases such as MongoDB, CouchDB or ElasticSearch, you will just let your application magically build a schema. Either way, you need to create a plan - even if it is on a napkin. This book will assume a traditional relational database is storing your data, but the principles are easily adapted for NoSQL systems too.

This chapter assumes you have already got a database designed and built. This chapter skips the "planning a database" section, because there are plenty of other books on that already.

1.2 Introduction to Database Seeding

With a database schema designed and implemented, the next step is to store some data. Instead of entering your real data, it is far easier to use "dummy data" to test if the schema is appropriate for your API application. This brings the added benefit of letting you ditch the database and try again without worrying about maintaining the data.

The process of populating a database is known as "seeding".

This data could be:

- test users
- content entries with a bunch of comments

- fake locations available for check-in
- fake notifications to display in an iPhone app (one of each type)
- credit-card payments at various stages of processing – with some complete, some half done and some super-fraudulent looking ones

The process of creating seeding scripts means you can avoid wasting time creating them manually over and over again. Ultimately, the more processes you can automate during the development of your API, the more time you have to consider the intricacies of your applications, which need much more consideration.

Dummy data is necessary for realistic acceptance testing, getting free-lancers/new hires up to speed with useful content, keeping real customer data private to those outside your company, and avoiding the temptation to copy live data over to your development environments.

Why is using production data in development bad?

Have you ever been writing a script that sends out emails and used some dummy copy while you're building it? Ever used some cheeky words in that content? Ever accidentally sent that email out to 10,000 real customers email addresses? Ever been fired for losing a company over £200,000?

I haven't, but I know a guy that has been. Don't be that guy.

What data should you use?

Garbage! Use absolute nonsense for your development database, but non-sense of the correct data type, size, and format. That can be done with a fun little library called Faker[1] by François Zaninotto[2] which is a wonderful little library that can essentially bullshit for Queen and country.

---

[1]https://github.com/fzaninotto/Faker
[2]https://twitter.com/francoisz/

1.3 Building Seeders

Kapture, the company I previously worked for, used the Laravel framework, which has Database Seeding[3] baked in. This is essentially a tarted up CLI task, which almost any modern PHP framework will have (or bloody well should), so the principles are applicable to all.

Break your database seeders down into logical groupings. This does not need to be "one seeder-per-table", but it can be. Sometimes your data needs to be built at the same time as other types of data. For example, users are created in the same seeder as their settings, OAuth tokens, and friendship data is made. Putting that into multiple seeders purely to keep things tidy would complicate your seeders and slow things down a lot, so maybe consider combining them.

In this chapter I will use a check-in application as an example. The application handles "users" and tracks their "check-ins" into "merchants" (or "venues"). "Merchants" also provide "campaigns" (or "opportunities").

So, this is a simplified version of the user seeder, ignoring the Laravel-specific structure. *If you are using Laravel, just shove this in your* `run()` *method.*

Creating a user with Faker and Eloquent ORM

```
1  $faker = Faker\Factory::create();
2
3  for ($i = 0; $i < Config::get('seeding.users'); $i++) {
4
5      $user = User::create([
6          'name' => $faker->name,
7          'email' => $faker->email,
8          'active' => $i === 0 ? true : $faker->boolean,
9          'gender' => $faker->randomElement(['male', 'female', 'other']),
10         'timezone' => $faker->numberBetween(-10, 10),
11         'birthday' => $faker->dateTimeBetween('-40 years', '-18 years'),
12         'location' => $faker->boolean ? "{$faker->city}, {$faker->state}" : null,
13         'had_feedback_email' => $faker->boolean,
14         'sync_name_bio' => $faker->boolean,
15         'bio' => $faker->sentence(100),
```

[3]http://laravel.com/docs/migrations#database-seeding

```
16        ]);
17    }
```

What do we have here? Let's go through this one section at a time:

```
1    $faker = Faker\Factory::create();
```

An instance of Faker, our bullshit artist for-hire.

```
3    for ($i = 0; $i < Config::get('seeding.users'); $i++) {
```

We are going to want a certain number of users, but you should have a few less on development than you do on testing or staging to save time.

```
5        $user = User::create([
6            'name' => $faker->name,
7            'email' => $faker->email,
```

Make a random name and random email. There is no need to define the pool of random data it uses, because IT'S MAGIC!

```
8            'active' => $i === 0 ? true : $faker->boolean,
```

Ok I lied, our garbage is not 100% random. We want user number 1 to be active for tests later on.

```
9            'gender' => $faker->randomElement(['male', 'female', 'other']),
```

Gender equality is important.

```
10           'timezone' => $faker->numberBetween(-10, 10),
```

Our original developer decided that saving time zones as an integer was a clever thing to do.

Store Time zones, Not Offsets

Did you know that some time zones are not complete hours? Did you know that Nepal is UTC/GMT +05:45? Did you know that Chatham Island (New Zealand) goes from UTC/GMT +12:45 to UTC/GMT +13:45 in their local summer? Did you know that some places add 30 minutes when in daylight savings time? Don't use integers as timestamps. Most major programming languages (PHP included) implement the IANA[4] time zone database, which is an industry standard. If you store `America/New_York` or `Asia/Khandyga` then the offset and daylight savings time can be automatically calculated.

```
11      'birthday' => $faker->dateTimeBetween('-40 years', '-18 years'),
```

Users of all of our target age demographic.

```
13      'location' => $faker->boolean ? "{$faker->city}, {$faker->state}" : null,
```

Give us a city name and a state name. This works fine with loads of countries, which is cool.

```
14      'had_feedback_email' => $faker->boolean,
15      'sync_name_bio' => $faker->boolean,
```

Some user flags are not as important, so set them to be `true` or `false` at random.

```
16      'bio' => $faker->sentence(100),
```

Make a sentence with 100 characters in it.

---

[4]http://www.iana.org/time-zones

1.4 That is about it

You will end up making a lot of these files, and you will want to populate
pretty much every table you have with data. You will also want to tell
your Database Seeder to wipe all the tables that will be populated. Do this
globally right at the start of the process. Do not wipe tables at the top of
each seeder, or content in that table from other seeders will be deleted.

Example of an overall system in Laravel

```
1   class DatabaseSeeder extends Seeder
2   {
3       public function run()
4       {
5           if (App::environment() === 'production') {
6               exit('I just stopped you getting fired. Love Phil');
7           }
8
9           // Disable mass-assignment protection with Laravel
10          Eloquent::unguard();
11
12          $tables = [
13              'locations',
14              'merchants',
15              'opps',
16              'opps_locations',
17              'moments',
18              'rewards',
19              'users',
20              'oauth_sessions',
21              'notifications',
22              'favorites',
23              'settings',
24              'friendships',
25              'impressions',
26          ];
27
28          foreach ($tables as $table) {
29              DB::table($table)->truncate();
30          }
31
32          $this->call('MerchantTableSeeder');
```

```
33          $this->call('PlaceTableSeeder');
34          $this->call('UserTableSeeder');
35          $this->call('OppTableSeeder');
36          $this->call('MomentTableSeeder');
37      }
38  }
```

This wipes everything, then runs other seeder classes to do their thing.

 Foreign Keys

It can be difficult to wipe a database when foreign keys constraints are enforced, so in that scenario your seeder should run `DB::statement('SET FOREIGN_KEY_CHECKS=0;');` before the truncation of the tables and `DB::statement('SET FOREIGN_KEY_CHECKS=1;');` afterwards to enable the checks again.

1.5 Secondary Data

As I said, it is quite likely that you will need to insert data that relates to itself. To do this, work out which data will be primary (like users). In the case of a check-in system you will also probably consider "venues" or "merchants", depending on the nomenclature of your system.

For this example, I will show how to create "merchants", then attach "opportunities", which are essentially "campaigns".

Primary Seeder for the Merchant Table

```php
1   <?php
2
3   class MerchantTableSeeder extends Seeder
4   {
5       /**
6        * Run the database seeds.
7        *
8        * @return void
9        */
10      public function run()
```

```
11   {
12       $faker = Faker\Factory::create();
13
14       // Create however many merchants
15       for ($i = 0; $i < Config::get('seeding.merchants'); $i++) {
16           Merchant::create([
17               'name'        => $faker->company,
18               'website'     => $faker->url,
19               'phone'       => $faker->phoneNumber,
20               'description' => $faker->text(200),
21           ]);
22       }
23   }
24 }
```

Primary Seeder for the Opp Table

```
1  <?php
2
3  use Carbon\Carbon;
4  use Kapture\CategoryFinder;
5
6  class OppTableSeeder extends Seeder
7  {
8      protected $categoryFinder;
9      protected $places;
10
11     public function __construct(CategoryFinder $finder, Place $places)
12     {
13         $this->categoryFinder = $finder;
14         $this->places = $places;
15     }
16
17     protected $imageArray = [
18         'http://example.com/images/example1.jpg',
19         'http://example.com/images/example2.jpg',
20         'http://example.com/images/example3.jpg',
21         'http://example.com/images/example4.jpg',
22         'http://example.com/images/example5.jpg',
23     ];
24
25     public function run()
```

```
26          {
27              $faker = Faker\Factory::create();
28
29              foreach (Merchant::all() as $merchant) {
30
31                  // Create however many opps for this merchant
32                  foreach (range(1, rand(2, 4)) as $i) {
33
34                      // There are three types of image to add
35                      $image = Image::create([
36                          'name' => "{$merchant->name} Image #{$i}",
37                          'url' => $faker->randomElement($this->imageArray),
38                      ]);
39
40                      // Start it immediately and make it last for 2 months
41                      $starts = Carbon::now();
42
43                      // We need to definitely have at least one we are in control of
44                      if ($i === 1) {
45                          // Have ONE that ends really soon
46                          $ends = Carbon::now()->addDays(2);
47                          $teaser = 'Something about cheese';
48
49                      } else {
50                          $ends = Carbon::now()->addDays(60);
51                          $teaser = $faker->sentence(rand(3, 5));
52                      }
53
54                      $category = $this->categoryFinder->setRandom()->getOne();
55
56                      $opp = Opp::create([
57                          'name'          => $faker->sentence(rand(3, 5)),
58                          'teaser'        => $teaser,
59                          'details'       => $faker->paragraph(3),
60                          'starts'        => $starts->format('Y-m-d H:i:s'),
61                          'ends'          => $ends->format('Y-m-d H:i:s'),
62                          'category_id'   => $category->id,
63                          'merchant_id'   => $merchant->id,
64                          'published'     => true,
65                      ]);
66
67                      // Attach an image to the opp
68                      $opp->images()->attach($image, [
```

```
69                      'published' => true
70                  ]);
71              }

73          echo "Created $i Opps for $merchant->name \n";
74      }
75    }
76 }
```

This might look a little crazy, and it is certainly a mixture of lazy-static ORM usage in the controller and some dependency injection, but these seeders have not received a large amount of love. They definitely do their job, and could always be cleaner, but here are the basics:

```
41          foreach (Merchant::all() as $merchant) {
```

Loop through all merchants.

```
43              // Create however many opps for this merchant
44              foreach (range(1, rand(2, 4)) as $i) {
```

Create between 1 and 4 opportunities for a merchant.

```
46                  // There are three types of image to add
47                  $image = Image::create([
48                      'name' => "{$merchant->name} Image #{$i}",
49                      'url' => $faker->randomElement($this->imageArray),
50                  ]);
```

Add an image from our array of example images on S3, or our website somewhere. The more the merrier.

```
66                  $category = $this->categoryFinder->setRandom()->getOne();
```

I will talk more about finders in a later chapter, but for now, just know this is a convenient way of getting a single random category back.

The rest should all be relatively obvious.

If you are using Laravel, you can run the above commands on the command line with: $ `php artisan db:seed`. The Rails equivalent is hilariously similar: $ `rake db:seed`.

1.6 When to run this?

Database seeds are often run both manually and automatically, depending on what is going on.

For example, if you have just added a new endpoint with new data, you will want to let your teammates know to pull the latest code, run the migrations and run the seed.

This is also great when a freelancer comes in to do some work, or a new developer starts up, or your iPhone dev wants to get some data to use. In all these instances, that command just needs to be run on the command line.

This is also occasionally run manually on the staging server and automatically on the Jenkins testing server when we deploy new builds of the API.

2. Planning and Creating Endpoints

With your database planned and full of fake but useful data it is time to plan what your endpoints are going to look like. An endpoint is simply a URL. When you go to `http://example.com/foo/bar` that is an endpoint and you can simply call it `/foo/bar` because the domain will be the same for all of them.

The first step is to work out the requirements of an API, then we can move onto some theory and finally see the theory implemented in some examples.

2.1 Functional Requirements

Try thinking of *everything* your API will need to handle. This will initially be a list of CRUD (create, read, update, delete) endpoints for your resources. Talk to your mobile app developer, your JS front-end people, or just talk to yourself if you are the only developer on the project.

Definitely talk to your customers or "the business" (they are the customers) and get them to help you think of functionality too, but they will probably not know what an endpoint is.

When you have a relatively extensive list the next step is to make a simple list of "actions". This is very much like planning a PHP class. You first write up pseudo-code referencing the classes and methods like they exist, right? TDD (Test Driven Development)? If not, that is how you should do it, or Chris Hartjes[1] will find you, and he *will* kill you.

I will go ahead with the check-in application, introduced in the previous chapter, to show how these principles can be put in practice.

If I have a "places" resource in mind, I need to list out with just bullet points what it will do:

---

[1]http://grumpy-learning.com/

Places
- **Create**
- **Read**
- **Update**
- **Delete**

That is fairly obvious. Who will be able to view these places and who will be able to create and edit them is, for now, irrelevant in our planning stages. This API will get much smarter with the ideas of user-context and permissions at a later date. For now, just list all the things that need to be done.

A paginate-able list of places is also a requirement, so get that down:

Places
- Create
- Read
- Update
- Delete
- **List**

The API will need to offer the ability to search places by location too, but that is not a brand new endpoint. If the API was built with SOAP or XML-RPC, you would create a `getPlacesByLatAndLon` method to hit in the URL, but this isn't SOAP - thankfully. The list method will handle that with a few parameters, so why not shove them in as a note for later:

Places
- Create
- Read
- Update
- Delete
- List **(lat, lon, distance or box)**

Adding a few parameters as a reminder, at this stage, is cool, but lets not worry about adding too much. For example, Create and Update are complicated, so adding every single field would be a mess.

Update is more than just updating the specific Places fields in a `places` SQL table. Update can do all sorts of cool stuff. If you need to "favorite" a Place, just send `is_favorite` to that endpoint and you've favorited it. More on that later, just remember that not every single action requires its own endpoint.

Places will also need to have an image uploaded via the API. In this example, we are only going to accept one image for a place and a new image overrides the old, so add "Image" to the list. Otherwise you'd add "Images" to the list:

    Places
    - Create
    - Read
    - Update
    - Delete
    - List (lat, lon, distance or box)
    - **Image**

A complete API action plan might look like this:

    Categories
    - Create
    - List

    Checkins
    - Create
    - Read
    - Update
    - Delete
    - List
    - Image

    Opps
    - Create
    - Read
    - Update

- Delete
- List
- Image
- Checkins

Places
- Create
- Read
- Update
- Delete
- List (lat, lon, distance or box)
- Image

Users
- Create
- Read
- Update
- Delete
- List (active, suspended)
- Image
- Favorites
- Checkins
- Followers

That might not contain everything, but it seems like a fairly solid start to our API. It is certainly going to take long enough to write all that, so if somebody thinks of something else they can just make an Issue.

Moving on.

2.2 Endpoint Theory

Turning this action plan into actual endpoints requires knowing a little theory on RESTful APIs and best practices for naming conventions. There are no right answers here, but some approaches have fewer cons than others. I will try to push you in the direction I have found to be most useful, and highlight the pros and cons of each.

GET Resources

- `GET /resources` – Some paginated list of stuff, in some logical default order, for that specific data.
- `GET /resources/X` – Just entity X. That can be an ID, hash, slug, username, etc., as long as it's unique to one "resource".
- `GET /resources/X,Y,Z` – The client wants multiple things, so give them multiple things.

It can be hard to pick between subresource URLs or embedded data. Embedded data can be rather difficult to pull off so that will be saved for Chapter 7: Embedding Data. For now the answer is "just subresources", but eventually the answer will be "both". This is how subresources look:

- `GET /places/X/checkins` – Find all the checkins for a specific place.
- `GET /users/X/checkins` – Find all the checkins for a specific user.
- `GET /users/X/checkins/Y` – Find a specific checkin for a specific user.

The latter is questionable and not something I have ever personally done. At that point, I would prefer to simply use `/checkins/X`.

 ## Auto-Increment is the Devil

In these examples X and Y can be an auto-incrementing ID as many developers will assume. One important factor with auto-incrementing ID's is that anyone with access to your API will know exactly how many resources you have, which might not be a statistic you want your competitors to have.

Consumers could also write a script which hits `/users/1`, then `/users/2` and `/users/3`, etc., scraping all data as it goes. Sure they could probably do that from the "list" endpoints anyway, but not all resources should have a "get all" approach.

Instead a unique identifier is often a good idea. A universal unique identifier (UUID) seems like a logical thing to do: ramsey\uuid for PHP[2], uuid for Ruby[3], uuid in Python 2.5+[4].

---

[2]https://github.com/ramsey/uuid
[3]https://rubygems.org/gems/uuid
[4]http://docs.python.org/2/library/uuid.html

DELETE Resources

Want to delete things? Easy:

- DELETE /places/X – Delete a single place.
- DELETE /places/X,Y,Z – Delete a bunch of places.
- DELETE /places – This is a potentially dangerous endpoint that could be skipped, as it should delete all places.
- DELETE /places/X/image – Delete the image for a place, or:
- DELETE /places/X/images – If you chose to have multiple images this would remove all of them.

POST vs PUT: FIGHT!

What about creating and updating? This is where it gets almost religious. There are lots of people who will try to pair the HTTP POST or HTTP PUT verb (verb, i.e. an HTTP method) to a specific CRUD action and always only ever do that one action with that one verb. That sucks and is not productive or functionally scalable.

Generally speaking, PUT is used if you know the entire URL beforehand and the action is idempotent. Idempotent is a fancy word for "can do it over and over again without causing different results".

For example, create *could* be a PUT if you are creating one image for a place. If you were to do this:

```
1  PUT /places/1/image HTTP/1.1
2  Host: example.com
3  Content-Type: image/jpeg
```

That would be a perfect example of when to use a PUT because you already know the entire URL (/places/1/image) and you can do it time and time again.

The API at Kapture used a POST to /checkins to create the metadata for that new check-in, then returned the URL for us to PUT the image to. You could try checking in multiple times and it would not matter because none of those processes would be complete, but POSTing multiple times is not idempotent because each checkin is different. PUT is idempotent because you are uploading that image to the full URL and you can do it over and over again if you like (for instance, because the upload failed and it has to try again).

So, if you have multiple images for places, maybe you could use the following:

    POST /places/X/images

Then multiple attempts would be different images. If you know you are only going to have one image and a new attempt is an override, then the following would be ideal:

    PUT /places/X/image

Another example could be user settings:

- POST /me/settings – I would expect this to allow me to POST specific fields one at a time, not force me to send the entire body of settings.
- PUT /me/settings – Send me ALL the settings.

It's a tricky difference, but do not try and tie an HTTP Method to one CRUD action only.

Plural, Singular or Both?

Some developers decide to make all endpoints singular, but I take issue with this. Given /user/1 and /user, which user is that last one returning? Is it "me"? What about /place? It returns multiple? Confusing.

I know it can be tempting to create /user/1 and /users because the two endpoints do different things, right? I started off down this route (#pun) originally, but in my experience, this convention grows badly. Sure it works with the example of "users", but what about those fun English words that create exceptions like /opportunity/1 which when pluralised becomes /opportunities. Gross.

I pick plural for everything as it is the most obvious:

- `/places` – "If I run a GET on that, I will get a collection of places"
- `/places/45` – "Pretty sure I am just talking about place 45"
- `/places/45,28` – "Ahh, places 45 and 28, got it"

Another solid reason for using plural consistently is that it allows for consistently named subresources:

- `/places`
- `/places/45`
- `/places/45/checkins`
- `/places/45/checkins/91`
- `/checkins/91`

Consistency is key.

Verb or Noun?

Traditionally APIs would consist of a series of endpoints that described actions:

```
1  POST /SendUserMessage HTTP/1.1
2  Host: example.com
3  Content-Type: application/x-www-form-urlencoded
4
5  id=5&message=Hello!
```

As you might have already gathered, this is not how things are done with REST.

Some API developers consider the following approach to be more RESTful because it uses a subresource:

```
1  POST /users/5/send-message HTTP/1.1
2  Host: example.com
3  Content-Type: application/json
4
5  { "message" : "Hello!" }
```

Nope, because that is still using a verb in the URL. A verb is an action – a doing term – and our API only needs one verb – the HTTP Method. All other verbs need to stay out of the URL.

A noun is a *place* or a *thing*. Resources are things, and a URL becomes the place on the Internet where a thing lives.

This example would be drastically more RESTful:

```
1  POST /users/5/messages HTTP/1.1
2  Host: example.com
3  Content-Type: application/json
4
5  { "message" : "Hello!" }
```

Perfect! We are creating a new message that belongs to a user. The best part about keeping it nice and RESTful like this is that other HTTP actions can be made to the identical URL:

- GET /users/philsturgeon/messages
- PATCH /users/philsturgeon/messages/xdWRwerG
- DELETE /users/philsturgeon/messages/xdWRwerG

This is all much easier to document and much easier to understand for both humans and software which is "RESTfully aware."

If, like a freelance client I consulted, you need to send multiple messages to multiple users (potentially hundreds of thousands) you could even make messages its own endpoint and send the messages in batches of a few hundred:

```
1   POST /messages HTTP/1.1
2   Host: example.com
3   Content-Type: application/json
4
5   [
6           {
7                   "user" : { "id" : 10 },
8                   "message" : "Hello!"
9           },
10          {
11                  "user" : { "username" : "philsturgeon" },
12                  "message" : "Hello!"
13          }
14  ]
```

It would look incredibly similar to create the data as it would to retrieve the data, which is intentional.

2.3 Planning Endpoints

Controllers

You need to list events, venues, users and categories? Easy. One controller for each type of resource:

- CategoriesController
- EventsController
- UsersController
- VenuesController

Everything should be a resource, and each resource needs a controller.

Later on we will look at some things that are not resources. Subresources can sometimes just be a method. For example, profile and settings are a subresource of users, so maybe they can go in UsersController. These rules are flexible.

Routes

Try to avoid the temptation to screw around with magic routing conventions[5], it is best to just write them manually. I will keep going with the previous examples and show the process of turning the action plan into routes using Laravel syntax, because why not:

Action	Endpoint	Route
Create	POST /users	Route::post('users', 'UsersController@create');
Read	GET /users/X	Route::get('users/{id}', 'UsersController@show');
Update	PUT /users/X	Route::put('users/{id}', 'UsersController@update');
Delete	DELETE /users/X	Route::delete('users/{id}', 'UsersController@delete');
List	GET /users	Route::get('users', 'UsersController@list');
Image	PUT /users/X/image	Route::put('users/{id}/image', 'UsersController@uploadImage');
Favorites	GET /users/X/favorites	Route::get('users/{id}/favorites', 'UsersController@favorites');
Checkins	GET /users/X/checkins	Route::get('users/{user_id}/checkins', 'CheckinsController@index');

There are a few things in here worth considering.

1. Favorites go to the `UserController` because favorites are only ever relevant to the user.
2. Checkins go to the `CheckinController` because we might already have a checkin controller handling `/checkins` and the logic is basically identical. We will know if there is a `user_id` param in the URL if our router is nice enough to let us know, so we can use that to make it user specific if needs be.

They are rather complex concerns, but are examples of things you can be thinking about at this point. You want to avoid having multiple endpoints doing painfully similar things with copy and paste logic because:

---

[5]https://philsturgeon.uk/blog/2013/07/beware-the-route-to-evil

1. PHP Copy/Paste Detector[6] will be angry.
2. Your iPhone developer will be mad that different endpoints provide the same resource, but in a slightly different format, therefore confusing RestKit.
3. It is boring and "ain't nobody got time for that!"

Methods

When you have listed all of the routes you will need for your application, go and make the corresponding controller methods. Make them all empty and have one of them `return "Oh hai!";`, and check the output. `GET /places` for example should `Oh hai!` in the browser.

You just wrote an API.

---

[6]https://github.com/sebastianbergmann/phpcpd

3. Input and Output Theory

3.1 Introduction

Now that we have a good idea of how endpoints work, the next glass of theory to swallow down is "input" and "output". This is the easiest of all, as it's really just HTTP "requests" and "responses". This is the same as AJAX or anything else.

If you have ever been forced to work with SOAP, you will know all about WSDLs. If you know what they are, be happy you no longer need them. If you do not know what a WSDL is, then be happy you never have to learn. SOAP was the worst.

Input is purely an HTTP request, and there are multiple parts to this.

3.2 Requests

```
1  GET /places?lat=40.759211&lon=-73.984638 HTTP/1.1
2  Host: api.example.com
```

This is a very simple GET request. We can see the URL path being requested is /places with a query string of lat=40.759211&lon=-73.984638. The HTTP version in use is HTTP/1.1; the host name is defined. This is essentially what your browser does when you go to any website - rather boring I'm sure.

```
1  POST /moments/1/gift HTTP/1.1
2  Host: api.example.com
3  Authorization: Bearer vr5HmMkzlxKE70W1y4MibiJUusZwZC25NOVBEx3BD1
4  Content-Type: application/json
5
6  { "user_id" : 2 }
```

Here we make a POST request with an "HTTP body". The `Content-Type` header points out we are sending JSON and the blank line above the JSON separates the "HTTP headers" from the "HTTP body". HTTP really is amazingly simple. This is all you need to do for anything, and you can do all of this with an HTTP client in whatever programming language you feel like using this week:

Using PHP and the Guzzle HTTP library to make an HTTP Request

```php
1   use Guzzle\Http\Client;
2
3   $headers = [
4       'Authorization' => 'Bearer vr5HmMkzlxKE70W1y4MibiJUusZwZC25NOVBEx3BD1',
5       'Content-Type' => 'application/json',
6   ];
7   $payload = [
8       'user_id' => 2
9   ];
10
11  // Create a client and provide a base URL
12  $client = new Client('http://api.example.com');
13
14  $req = $client->post('/moments/1/gift', $headers, json_encode($payload));
```

Using Python and the Requests HTTP library to make an HTTP Request

```python
1   import json
2   import requests
3
4   headers = {
5       'Authorization': 'Bearer vr5HmMkzlxKE70W1y4MibiJUusZwZC25NOVBEx3BD1',
6       'Content-Type': 'application/json',
7   }
8   payload = {
9       'user_id': 2
10  }
11  req = requests.post(
12    'http://api.example.com/moments/1/gift',
13    data=json.dumps(payload),
14    headers=headers
15  )
```

It's all the same. Define your headers, define the body in an appropriate format, and send it on its way. Then you get a response; so let's talk about that.

3.3 Responses

Much the same as an HTTP Request, your HTTP Response is going to end up as plain text (unless you're using SSL, but shut up, we aren't there yet).

Example HTTP response containing a JSON body

```
1   HTTP/1.1 200 OK
2   Server: nginx
3   Content-Type: application/json
4   Connection: close
5   X-Powered-By: PHP/5.5.5-1+debphp.org~quantal+2
6   Cache-Control: no-cache, private
7   Date: Fri, 22 Nov 2013 16:37:57 GMT
8   Transfer-Encoding: Identity
9
10  {
11    "id":"1690",
12    "is_gift":true,
13    "user":{
14      "id":1,
15      "name":"Theron Weissnat",
16      "bio":"Occaecati excepturi magni odio distinctio dolores.",
17      "gender":"female",
18      "picture_url":"https:\/\/cdn.example.com/foo.png",
19      "timezone":-1,
20      "birthday":"1989-09-17 16:27:36",
21      "status":"available",
22      "created_at":"2013-11-22 16:37:57",
23      "redeem_by":"2013-12-22 16:37:57"
24    }
25  }
```

We can spot some fairly obvious things here. 200 OK is a standard no-issues-here-buddy response. We have a Content-Type again, and the API is pointing out that caching this is not ok. The X-Powered-By header is also a nice little reminder that I should switch `expose_php = On` to `expose_php = Off` in php.ini. Oops.

This is essentially the majority of how an API works. Just like learning a programming language, you will always come across new functions and utilities that will improve the RESTful-ness of your API. I will point out a bunch of them as we go, but just like the levenshtein()[1] function in PHP, there will be HTTP Headers that you had no idea existed popping up that will make you think, "How the shit did I not notice that?".

3.4 Supporting Formats

Picking what formats to support is hard, but there are a few easy wins to make early on.

No Form Data

PHP developers always try to do something that literally nobody else does, and that is to send form data to the API using the `application/x-www-form-urlencoded` content type.

This content type is one of the few ways that browsers send data via a form when you use HTTP POST, and PHP will take that data, slice it up, and make it available in `$_POST`. Because of this convenient feature, many PHP developers will make their API send data that way. Later they wonder why sending data with PUT is "different" and wonder why there is no `$_PUT` in PHP.

Urf.

`$_GET` and `$_POST` do not have the 1:1 relationship with HTTP GET and HTTP POST as their names might suggest. `$_GET` just contains query string content *regardless* of the HTTP method. `$_POST` contains the values of the HTTP Body if it was in the right format, and the `Content-Type` header is `application/x-www-form-urlencoded`. An HTTP POST item could still have a query string, and that would still be in `$_GET`. Some PHP frameworks kill off `$_GET` data in an HTTP POST request, which further exaggerates this 1:1 relationship between the superglobal and the method.

---

[1]http://php.net/manual/en/function.levenshtein.php

Knowing that PHP has some silly names for things, we can move on and completely ignore $_POST. Pour one out in the ground, because it is dead to you.

Why? So many reasons, including the fact that once again everything in application/x-www-form-urlencoded is a string.

```
1   foo=something&bar=1&baz=0
```

Yeah, you have to use 1 or 0 because bar=true would be string("true") on the server-side. Data types are important, so let's not just throw them out the window for the sake of "easy access to our data". That argument is also moronic as something like Input::json('foo') is possible in most decent PHP frameworks. Even without it, you just have to use file_get_contents('php://input') to read the HTTP body yourself.

php://input on < PHP 5.6

In versions of PHP prior to 5.6 the input stream would empty after first read. Basically, if you tried to read the HTTP body twice, the second attempt would fail. This has been fixed in PHP 5.6.0 so feel free to hit it as many times as you like.

```
1   POST /checkins HTTP/1.1
2   Host: api.example.com
3   Authorization: Bearer vr5HmMkzlxKE70W1y4MibiJUusZwZC25NOVBEx3BD1
4   Content-Type: application/json
5
6   {
7       "checkin": {
8           "place_id" : 1,
9           "message": "This is a bunch of text.",
10          "with_friends": [1, 2, 3, 4, 5]
11      }
12  }
```

This is a perfectly valid HTTP body for a checkin. You know what they are saying. You know who the user is from their auth token. You know who they are with and you get the benefit of having it wrapped up in a single `checkin` key for simple documentation, and, easy "You sent a checkin object to the user settings page, muppet." responses.

That same request using form data is a mess.

```
1  POST /checkins HTTP/1.1
2  Host: api.example.com
3  Authorization: Bearer vr5HmMkzlxKE70W1y4MibiJUusZwZC25NOVBEx3BD1
4  Content-Type: application/x-www-form-urlencoded
5
6  checkin[place_id]=1&checkin[message]=This is a bunch of text&checkin[with_friends][]=\
7  1&checkin[with_friends][]=2&checkin[with_friends][]=3&checkin[with_friends][]=4&check\
8  in[with_friends][]=5
```

This makes me upset *and* angry. Do not do it in your API.

Finally, do not try to be clever by mixing JSON with form data:

```
1   POST /checkins HTTP/1.1
2   Host: api.example.com
3   Authorization: Bearer vr5HmMkzlxKE70W1y4MibiJUusZwZC25NOVBEx3BD1
4   Content-Type: application/x-www-form-urlencoded
5
6   json="{
7       \"checkin\": {
8           \"place_id\" : 1,
9           \"message\": \"This is a bunch of text.\",
10          \"with_friends\": [1, 2, 3, 4, 5]
11      }
12  }"
```

Who is the developer trying to impress with stuff like that? It is insanity, and anyone who tries this needs to have their badge and gun revoked.

Developers do this because they still want "easy access" to their JSON, but do not know how to read it from the HTTP Body correctly.

Sending proper JSON data is rather simple in most server-side languages as demonstrated at the start of this chapter, but JavaScript can be a little different. If you are working with frameworks, like Backbone, EmberJS and AngularJS, then they will most likely be handling their data interactions with your API in JSON already.

If you need to do this manually, you can use jQuery's `$.ajax()` method:

```
1  $.ajax({
2    type: "POST",
3    url: url,
4    data: { foo : "bar" },
5    success: success,
6    dataType: "json"
7  });
```

This is a very manual approach, which may be too time consuming, so jQuery has another solution. The `$.serializeArray()` method[2] can turn values from all matched elements into a JSON string for you to then send to the API.

JSON and XML

Any modern API you interact with will support JSON unless it is a financial services API, or the developer is a moron – probably both to be fair. Sometimes they will support XML too. XML used to be the popular format for data transfer with both SOAP and XML-RPC (duh). XML is, however, a nasty-ass disgusting mess of tags, and the file-size of an XML file containing the same data as a JSON file is often much larger.

Beyond purely the size of the data being stored, XML is horribly bad at storing type. That might not worry a PHP developer all that much as PHP is not really any better when it comes to type, but look at this:

```
1  {
2      "place": {
3          "id" : 1,
4          "name": "This is a bunch of text.",
5          "is_true": false,
6          "maybe": null,
7          "empty_string": ""
8      }
9  }
```

That response in XML:

---

[2]http://api.jquery.com/serializearray/

```
1   <places>
2       <place>
3           <id>1</id>,
4           <name>This is a bunch of text.</name>
5           <is_true>0</is_true>
6           <maybe />
7           <empty_string />
8       </place>
9   </places>
```

Basically, in XML, *everything* is considered a string, meaning integers, booleans, and nulls can be confused. Both `maybe` and `empty_string` have the same value, because there is no way to denote a null value either. Gross.

Now, the XML-savvy among you will be wondering why I am not using attributes to simplify it? Well, this XML structure is a typical "auto-generated" chunk of XML converted from an array in the same way that JSON is built – but this of course ignores attributes and does not allow for all the specific structure that your average XML consumer will almost certainly demand.

If you want to start using attributes for some bits of data but not others, then your conversion logic becomes INSANELY complicated. How would we build something like this?

```
1   <places>
2       <place id="1" is_true="1">
3           <name>This is a bunch of text.</name>
4           <empty_string />
5       </place>
6   </places>
```

The answer is that unless you seek specific fields, try to guess that an "id" is probably an attribute, etc., then there is no programmatic way in your API to take the same array and make JSON *and* XML. Instead, you realistically need to use a "view" (from the MVC pattern) to represent this data, just like you would with HTML, or work with XML generation in a more OOP way. Either way, it is an abomination, and I refuse to work in those conditions. Luckily, nobody at Kapture wanted XML, so I did not have to rage quit back to England.

If your team is on the fence about XML, and you are not required by the business to use it, then skip it. It can be fun to show off your API switching formats and supporting all sorts of stuff (and we will get to that later on) but XML is a complication many APIs do not require these days.

Work out which format(s) you actually need, and *stick to those*. Sure Flickr supports lolcat as input and output, but they have a much bigger team, and that was probably the result of a hack project in which the development team were only paid with cold pizza. JSON is fine. If you have a lot of Ruby cool kids around, then you will probably want to output YAML too, which is as easy to generate as JSON in most cases.

3.5 Content Structure

This is a tough topic and there is no right answer. Whether you use EmberJS, RestKit, or any other framework with knowledge of REST, you will find somebody annoyed that the data is not in their specific preferred format. There are a lot of factors, and I will simply explain them all and let you know where I landed.

JSON-API

There is one recommended format on JSON-API[3], which maybe you all just want to use. It suggests that both single resources and resource collections should both be inside a plural key.

```
1  {
2    "posts": [{
3      "id": "1",
4      "title": "Rails is Omakase"
5    }]
6  }
```

Pros

- Consistent response – It *always* has the same structure

---

[3]http://jsonapi.org/format/

Cons

- Some RESTful/Data utilities freak about having single responses in an array
- Potentially confusing to humans

EmberJS (EmberData) used to have a rough time with JSON-API out of the box, but the EmberJS team and the JSON-API people have worked together to improve the situation. Rails and AngularJS also have a lot of people focusing on JSON-API as a centralized standard too, but it is not always perfect.

JSON-API is a wonderful resource with a lot of great ideas, but it strikes me as over complicated in multiple areas. It is also (in April 2015) still not v1.0.0 final. RC versions are released with breaking changes every few months, and this can be a huge problem for those with previous versions already implemented and live.

 Update 2015-05-29: JSON-API v1.0

To little fanfare, JSON-API v1.0 has finally been released. It has solved a few of problems in previous RC versions. As predicted, the switch to v1.0 created more than a few problems for developers of APIs who had already implemented earlier versions.
Luckily, at Ride, we were not requiring the `application/vnd.api+json` mime type, which means we can use this as a switch. If nothing is provided, we know it's our old API clients and default to JSON-API v1.0 RC2, but if that header is provided we can use a different adapter and serialize to JSON-API v1.0 final. A bit of a hack, but it works, and we do not have to implement versioning to do it.

Twitter-style

Ask for one user get one user:

```
1  {
2    "name": "Hulk Hogan",
3    "id": "100002"
4  }
```

Ask for a collection of things, get a collection of things:

```
1  [
2    {
3      "name": "Hulk Hogan",
4      "id": "100002"
5    },
6    {
7      "name": "Mick Foley",
8      "id": "100003"
9    }
10 ]
```

Pros

- Minimalistic response
- Almost every framework/utility can comprehend it

Cons

- No space for pagination or other metadata

This is potentially a reasonable solution if you will never use pagination or metadata.

Facebook-style

Ask for one user get one user:

```
1  {
2    "name": "Hulk Hogan",
3    "id": "100002"
4  }
```

Ask for a collection of things, get a collection of things, but namespaced:

```
1  {
2    "data": [
3      {
4        "name": "Hulk Hogan",
5        "id": "100002"
6      },
7      {
8        "name": "Mick Foley",
9        "id": "100003"
10     }
11   ]
12 }
```

Pros

- Space for pagination and other metadata in collection
- Simplistic response even with the extra namespace

Cons

- Single items still can only have metadata by embedding it in the item resource

By placing the collection into the `"data"` namespace, you can easily add other content next to it, which relates to the response, but is not part of the list of resources at all. Counts, links, etc., can all go here (more on this later). It also means when you embed other nested relationships you can include a "data" element for them and even include metadata for those embedded relationships. More on that later too.

The only potential "con" left with Facebook is that the single resources are not namespaced, meaning that adding any sort of metadata would pollute the global namespace – something which PHP developers are against after a decade of flagrantly doing so.

So the final output example (and the one which I used at Kapture for v4) is the following.

Much Namespace, **Nice Output**

Namespace the resource:

```
1  {
2    "data": {
3      "name": "Phil Sturgeon",
4      "id": "511501255"
5    }
6  }
```

Namespace the collection:

```
1  {
2    "data": [
3      {
4        "name": "Hulk Hogan",
5        "id": "100002"
6      },
7      {
8        "name": "Mick Foley",
9        "id": "100003"
10     }
11   ]
12 }
```

This is close to the JSON-API response. It has the benefits of the Facebook approach, and is just like Twitter, but everything is namespaced. Some folks (including me in the past) will suggest that you should change `"data"` to `"users"`, but when you start to nest your data, you want to keep that special name for the name of the relationship. For example:

```
 1  {
 2    "data": {
 3      "name": "Hulk Hogan",
 4      "id": "100002"
 5      "comments": {
 6          "data": [
 7              {
 8                 "id": 123423
 9                 "text": "Sorry I said those inappropriate things!"
10              }
11          ]
12      }
13    }
14  }
```

So here we can see the benefits of keeping the root scope generic. We know that a user is being returned, because we are requesting a user, and when comments are being returned we wrap that in a `"data"` item so that pagination, or links, can be added to that nested data too. This is the structure I will be testing against and using for examples, but it is only a simple tweak between any of these structures.

We will get to links, relationships, compound documents, pagination, etc., in later chapters, but for now forget about it. All you want to worry about is your response, which consists of this chunk of data or an error.

4. Status Codes, Errors and Messages

4.1 Introduction

If a valid request comes in for data, you show data. If creating something on the API with valid data, you show the created object. If something goes wrong, however, you want to let people know what is wrong using two simultaneous approaches:

1. HTTP status codes
2. Custom error codes and messages

4.2 HTTP Status Codes

Status codes are used in all responses and have a number from 200 to 507 – with plenty of gaps in between – and each has a message and a definition. Most server-side languages, frameworks, etc., default to 200 OK.

Status codes are grouped into a few different categories:

2xx is all about success

Whatever the client tried to do was successful up to the point that the response was sent. Keep in mind that a status like 202 Accepted does not say anything about the actual result, it only indicates that a request was accepted and is being processed asynchronously.

3xx is all about redirection

These are all about sending the calling application somewhere else for the actual resource. The best known of these are the 303 See Other and the 301 Moved Permanently, which are used a lot on the web to redirect a browser to another URL.

4xx is all about client errors

With these status codes, we indicate that the client has done something invalid and needs to fix the request before resending it.

5xx is all about service errors

With these status codes, we indicate that something went wrong in the service. For example, a database connection failed. Typically, a client application can retry the request. The server can even specify when the client is allowed to retry the command using a `Retry-After` HTTP header.

Using HTTP status codes in a REST service[1] – Maurice de Beijer

For a more complete list of HTTP status codes and their definitions the REST & WOA Wiki[2] has an extensive list of them.

Arguments between developers will continue for the rest of time over the exact appropriate code to use in any given situation, but these are the status codes the API used at Kapture:

- 200 – Generic everything is OK
- 201 – Created something OK
- 202 – Accepted but is being processed async (for a video means encoding, for an image means resizing, etc.)
- 400 – Bad Request (should really be for invalid syntax, but some folks use for validation)
- 401 – Unauthorized (no current user and there should be)
- 403 – The current user is forbidden from accessing this data
- 404 – That URL is not a valid route, or the item resource does not exist
- 405 – Method Not Allowed (your framework will probably do this for you)
- 410 – Data has been deleted, deactivated, suspended, etc.
- 500 – Something unexpected happened, and it is the APIs fault
- 503 – API is not here right now, please try again later

It can be tempting to try and squeeze as many error codes in as you can, but I would advise you to try and keep it simple. You won't unlock any achievement badges for using them all.

---

[1]http://www.develop.com/httpstatuscodesrest
[2]http://restpatterns.org/HTTP_Status_Codes

Most 5xx issues will likely happen under odd architecture or server related issues that are nothing to do with your API. For example, if PHP-FPM segfaults behind Nginx (502), if your Amazon Elastic Load Balancer has no healthy instances (503), or if your disk drive fills up with cat gifs (507).

4.3 Error Codes and Error Messages

Error codes are usually strings or integers that act as a unique index to a corresponding human-readable error message with more information about what is going wrong. That sounds a lot like HTTP status codes, but these errors are about application specific things that may or may not have anything to do with HTTP specific responses.

Some folks will try to use HTTP status codes exclusively and skip using error codes because they do not like the idea of making their own error codes or having to document them, but this is not a scalable approach. There will be some situations where the same endpoint could easily return the same status code for more than one different condition. The status codes are there to merely hint at the category of error relying on the actual error code and error message provided in the HTTP response to include more information in case the client is interested.

For example, an issue with the access token will always result in the user not being recognized. An uninterested client would simply say "User could not get in" while a more interested client would probably prefer to offer suggestions via messages in their own webapp/iPhone app interface.

```
1  {
2    "error": {
3      "type": "OAuthException",
4      "message": "Session has expired at unix time 1385243766.
5  The current unix time is 1385848532."
6    }
7  }
```

Humans can understand that nicely enough, but Facebook used to lack error codes, making it rather hard for computers to understand the problem. They have added them since the first edition of this book, but before that you would find yourself doing substring matching on the message text, which is lunacy.

Foursquare is not a bad example of using both, but they place an emphasis on tying their errors to a status code.

https://developer.foursquare.com/overview/responses

Twitter does a great job of having HTTP status codes documented and having specific error codes for other issues too. Some are tied to HTTP status codes, which is fine, but many are not. Some are also tied to the same status code, highlighting the issues raised above.

https://dev.twitter.com/docs/error-codes-responses

Code	Text	Description
161	You are unable to follow more people at this time	Corresponds with HTTP 403 – thrown when a user cannot follow another user due to some kind of limit
179	Sorry, you are not authorized to see this status	Corresponds with HTTP 403 – thrown when a Tweet cannot be viewed by the authenticating user, usually due to the tweet's author having protected their tweets.

Programmatically Detecting Error Codes

You can use error codes to make an application respond intelligently to failure of something as basic as a posted Twitter status.

Using Python to catch exceptions and react to the Twitter error code

```
1  try:
2      api.PostUpdates(body['text'])
3
4  except twitter.TwitterError, exc:
5
6      skip_codes = [
7          # Page does not exist
8          34,
9
```

```
10          # You cannot send messages to users who are not following you
11          150,
12
13          # Sent too many
14          # TODO Make this requeue with a dekal somehow
15          151
16      ]
17
18      error_code = exc.__getitem__(0)[0]['code']
19
20      # If the error code is one of those listed before, let's just end here
21      if error_code in skip_codes:
22          message.reject()
23
24      else:
25          # Rate limit exceeded? Might be worth taking a nap before we requeue
26          if error_code == 88:
27              time.sleep(10)
28
29          message.requeue()
```

Compare this sort of logic with the Facebook example from when they lacked error codes:

Using Python to analyse Facebook error strings as no codes exist

```
1   except facebook.GraphAPIError, e:
2
3       phrases = ['expired', 'session has been invalidated']
4
5       for phrase in phrases:
6
7           # If the token has expired then lets knock it out so we don't try again
8           if e.message.find(phrase) > 0:
9               log.info("Deactivating Token %s", user['token_id'])
10              self._deactivate_token(user['token_id'])
11
12       log.error("-- Unknown Facebook Error", exec_info=True)
```

If they change their error messages then this might stop working, which would be a problem. Codes that do not change are a much more sensible way to go about this.

If Facebook added codes and documentation links to GraphAPI error responses.

```
1  {
2    "error": {
3      "type": "OAuthException",
4      "code": "ERR-01234",
5      "message": "Session has expired at unix time 1385243766. The current unix time is\
6    1385848532."
7      "href": "http://example.com/docs/errors/#ERR-01234"
8    }
9  }
```

4.4 Error or Errors

When returning errors, I always used to return just one error. In the case of validation I would return them one at a time as an easy way to exit out of a controller. Thinking about it this was probably just laziness.

After being forced to work with the JSON-API standard, the use of multiple errors started to feel more natural.

If Facebook returned multiple errors in a list for GraphAPI responses.

```
1  {
2    "errors": [{
3      "type": "OAuthException",
4      "code": "ERR-01234",
5      "message": "Session has expired at unix time 1385243766. The current unix time is\
6    1385848532."
7      "href": "http://example.com/docs/errors/#ERR-01234"
8    }]
9  }
```

4.5 Standards for Error Responses

So far, this chapter has used entirely home-grown formats for errors. It is incredibly common, even with the most popular APIs to build completely arbitrary error formats, so I wanted to teach you the theory before forcing you to read complicated standards.

There are two popular standards that cover error reporting, which are both fairly similar, but sadly still in draft at time of writing.

JSON-API

JSON-API[3] is discussed in a few sections of this book and is a standard outlining the general format of requests and responses in JSON when working with HTTP APIs. It has a section on errors, which I quite like.

The following is an excerpt from the JSON-API standard at time of writing.

> An error object MAY have the following members:
>
> - `"id"` – A unique identifier for this particular occurrence of the problem.
> - `"href"` – A URI that MAY yield further details about this particular occurrence of the problem.
> - `"status"` – The HTTP status code applicable to this problem, expressed as a string value.
> - `"code"` – An application-specific error code, expressed as a string value.
> - `"title"` – A short, human-readable summary of the problem. It SHOULD NOT change from occurrence to occurrence of the problem, except for purposes of localization.
> - `"detail"` – A human-readable explanation specific to this occurrence of the problem.
> - `"links"` – Associated resources, which can be dereferenced from the request document.
> - `"path"` – The relative path to the relevant attribute within the associated resource(s). Only appropriate for problems that apply to a single resource or type of resource.
>
> Additional members MAY be specified within error objects.

When constructing your API error responses, you pretty much just need to make an array with items that looks a bit like this:

---

[3]http://jsonapi.org/format/#errors

```
1  {
2    "errors": [{
3      "code": "ERR-01234",
4      "title": "OAuth Exception",
5      "details": "Session has expired at unix time 1385243766. The current unix time is\
6  1385848532.",
7      "href": "http://example.com/docs/errors/#ERR-01234"
8    }]
9  }
```

See how that Facebook example has been slightly tweaked to follow the standard? Nice and easy.

Problem Details for HTTP APIs

This is currently a draft RFC[4], which at the time of writing was on Draft 7.

The goal of this RFC is to define a "problem detail", like we have been doing throughout this chapter, but in a standard way (to avoid inventing new formats for each and every HTTP API). It is being headed up by Mark Nottingham.

Mark wrote a tutorial about problem details[5], which will explain the standard a little better.

If you are interested in implementing this standard then there are tools to make it easy:

- crell/api-problem[6] for PHP

4.6 Common Pitfalls

200 OK and Error Code

If you return an HTTP status code of 200 with an error code, then Chuck Norris will roundhouse your door in, destroy your computer, instantly

---

[4]http://tools.ietf.org/html/draft-nottingham-http-problem
[5]https://www.mnot.net/blog/2013/05/15/http_problem
[6]https://github.com/Crell/ApiProblem

35-pass wipe your backups, cancel your Dropbox account, and block you from GitHub. HTTP 4xx or 5xx codes alert the client that something bad happened, and error codes provide specifics of the exact issue if the client is interested.

Non-Existent, Gone, or Hiding?

404 is drastically overused in APIs. People use it for "never existed", "no longer exists", "you can't view it" and "it is deactivated", which is way too vague. That can be split up into 404, 403 and 410 but this is still vague.

If you get a 403, this could be because the requesting user is not in the correct group to see the requested content. Should the client suggest you upgrade your account somehow? Are you not friends with the user whose content you are trying to view? Should the client suggest you add them as a friend?

A 410 on a resource could be due to a user deleting that entire piece of content, or it could be down to the user deleting their entire account.

In all of these situations, the ideal solution is to complement the HTTP status code with an error code, which can be whatever you want as long as they are unique within your API and documented somewhere.

Do not do what Google does — supply a list of error codes while having other error codes that are not documented *anywhere* — because if I see that, I will come for you.

5. Endpoint Testing

5.1 Introduction

You might be sitting there thinking, "This escalated quickly, I'm not ready for testing!" but this is essentially the point. You have to set up your tests as early as possible so you actually bother using them, otherwise they become the *next thing* that just never gets done. Have no fear. Testing an API is not only easy, it is actually really quite fun.

5.2 Concepts & Tools

With an API, there are a few things to test, but the most basic idea is, "when I request this URL, I want to see a foo resource", and "when I throw this JSON at the API, it should a) accept it or b) freak out."

This can be done in several ways, and a lot of people will instantly try to unit test it, but that quickly becomes a nightmare. While you might think just writing a bit of code with your favourite HTTP client is simple, if you have over 50 endpoints and want to do multiple checks per endpoint, you end up with a mess of code which can become hard to maintain, especially if your favourite HTTP client releases a major version with a brand new interface.

The more code you have in your tests, the higher the chances of your tests being rubbish, which means you won't run them. Bad tests also run the risk of false positives, which are super dangerous as they lead you into thinking your code actually works when it does not.

One very simplistic approach will be to use a BDD (Behaviour Driven Development) tool. A very popular BDD tool is Cucumber[1], and this is considered by many to be a Ruby tool. It can in fact be used for Python, PHP, and probably a whole bevy of other languages but some of the

---

[1] http://cukes.info/

integrations can be tricky. For the PHP users here, we will be using Behat, which is pretty much the same thing, along with Gherkin[2] (the same DSL (Domain-Specific Language) that Cucumber uses, so all of us are on basically the same page.)

The outline of this chapter will be to show how to set up and use the BDD tool Behat, talk through the various moving parts, then show you a working example in our source code inside a Laravel sample app. You can build your own tests in your own language, or in any framework, but just go along with this PHP example to see a basic working - even if you personally prefer another language. Go on. It won't bite.

5.3 Setup

As a PHP developer, you simply need to install Behat, which can be done with Composer[3]. It is fair to assume that if you are using any sort of modern PHP framework, you are already familiar with Composer, so we can skip boring the non-PHP developers by getting too stuck into it.

Assuming that Composer is installed globally[4] in your system, to install Behat run:

Install Behat globally with Composer

```
1  $ composer global require "behat/behat ~2.5"
```

Make sure ~/.composer/vendor/bin/ is added to your $PATH and you should be good to go.

If you are a Ruby user, you have the ease of simply running $ gem install cucumber, or shove it in your Gemfile.

Google should help you with Python.

The rest of this chapter is going to stick purely to PHP for the sake of simplicity, and others can just use the equivalent commands as we go.

---

[2]http://docs.behat.org/guides/1.gherkin.html
[3]https://getcomposer.org/
[4]https://getcomposer.org/doc/00-intro.md#globally

5.4 Initialise

These Behat tests will live in a `tests` folder, but it may need to coexist with other unit tests or other types of test. For this reason, I like to put them in a subfolder called `tests/behat`.

I have provided an example of a simple Behat test suite in the sample code that lives inside the `app/` folder. This is done mainly because it is a good place to put your tests and Laravel already has a tests folder, but if you are using any other framework you can put these tests anywhere you please.

So, go to the app folder:

```
1   $ cd ~/apisyouwonthate/chapter5/app
```

The folder structure and basic Behat setup has already been run with the following commands, so you can skip this step:

```
1   $ mkdir -p tests/behat && cd tests/behat
2   $ behat --init
```

This will have the following output:

```
1   +d features - place your *.feature files here
2   +d features/bootstrap - place bootstrap scripts and static files here
3   +f features/bootstrap/FeatureContext.php - place your feature related code here
```

The output here outlines the structure of files it has created. Everything lives inside the `features/` folder, and this will be where your Behat tests will go. The `features/bootstrap/` folder contains only one file at this point, which is `FeatureContext.php`.

The default version of this file is a little bare, so this sample code contains a beefed up one, which will be used throughout this chapter.

5.5 Features

Features are a way to group your various tests together. Personally, I keep things fairly simple and consider each resource and subresource to be its own Behat feature.

Looking at our users example from Chapter 2: Planning and Creating Endpoints:

Action	Endpoint	Feature
Create	POST /users	features/users.feature
Read	GET /users/X	features/users.feature
Update	PUT /users/X	features/users.feature
Delete	DELETE /users/X	features/users.feature
List	GET /users	features/users.feature
Image	PUT /users/X/image	features/users-image.feature
Favorites	GET /users/X/favorites	features/users-favorites.feature
Checkins	GET /users/X/checkins	features/users-checkins.feature

So, anything to do with /users and /users/X would be the same, but maybe /users/X/checkins becomes a new feature because we are talking about something else.

You can use that convention, or try something else, but this grows pretty well without having a bazillion files to sift through.

5.6 Scenarios

Gherkin uses "scenarios" as its core structure and they each contain "steps". In a unit testing world the scenarios would be their own test_- foo() methods, and the steps would be assertions.

These features and scenarios line up with the action plan created in Chapter 2. Each RESTful resource in that action plan needs at least one feature, and because each action has an endpoint we need *at least* one scenario for each action.

Too much jargon? Time for an example:

```
 1    Feature: Places
 2
 3    Scenario: Finding a specific place
 4        When I request "GET /places/1"
 5        Then I get a "200" response
 6        And scope into the "data" property
 7            And the properties exist:
 8                """
 9                id
10                name
11                lat
12                lon
13                address1
14                address2
15                city
16                state
17                zip
18                website
19                phone
20                """
21            And the "id" property is an integer
22
23    Scenario: Listing all places is not possible
24        When I request "GET /places"
25        Then I get a "400" response
26
27    Scenario: Searching non-existent places
28        When I request "GET /places?q=c800e42c377881f8ae509cf9a516d4eb59&lat=1&lon=1"
29        Then I get a "200" response
30        And the "data" property contains 0 items
31
32    Scenario: Searching places with filters
33        When I request "GET /places?lat=40.76855&lon=-73.9945&q=cheese"
34        Then I get a "200" response
35        And the "pagination" property is an object
36        And the "data" property is an array
37        And scope into the first "data" property
38            And the properties exist:
39                """
40                id
41                name
42                lat
43                lon
```

```
44              address1
45              address2
46              city
47              state
48              zip
49              website
50              phone
51              """
52      And reset scope
```

This uses some custom rules that have been defined in the file `FeatureContext.php`. More on that shortly.

The "feature file" is called `places.feature` and has four scenarios. One to find a specific place, another to show that listing all places is not allowed (400 means bad input, you should specify `lat` and `lon`), and two more to test how well searching works.

Try to think up the guard clauses that the endpoints will need, then make a scenario for each of those.

For example, if the endpoint requires `lat` and `lon` as query string parameters, try omitting them and testing that to ensure the error message and status codes are correct.

If an input is expecting a boolean value, but a string is provided? Maybe that should be a test too:

```
1   Scenario: Wrong Arguments for user follow
2       Given I have the payload:
3           """
4           {"is_following": "foo"}
5           """
6       When I request "PUT /users/1"
7       Then I get a "400" response
```

Want to be sure your controllers can handle weird requests with a 404 instead of freaking out and going all 500 Internal Error? There is another test:

```
1   Scenario: Try to find an invalid moments
2       When I request "GET /moments/nope"
3       Then I get a "404" response
```

Sure there is no actual code yet, but you can write all of these tests based off of nothing but your action plan and your routes. You should use what you know about the output content structure from Chapter 3 to plan what output you expect to see.

Then all you need to do is... you know... build your entire API.

5.7 Prepping Behat

You are probably wondering how you actually run these tests, because Behat involves making HTTP requests, and you've just been writing text-files. Well, the class in `FeatureContext.php` handles all of that and a lot more, but first we need to configure Behat so we know what the hostname is going to be for these requests.

```
1   $ vim app/tests/behat/behat-dev.yml
```

In this file put in something along the lines of:

```
1   default:
2     context:
3       parameters:
4           base_url: http://localhost:8000
```

If you have virtual hosts set up on your machine then use those, and if you are running a local web server on a different port, then obviously you can use that too. That value could be `http://localhost:4000` or `http://dev-api.example.com`, it does not matter.

5.8 Running Behat

This is the easiest bit:

```
1   $ behat -c tests/behat/behat-dev.yml
```

Running this from the sample application should return a lot of green lights, because I have gone to the effort of writing a few very basic feature tests against a few very simple endpoints that return data from a SQLite database.

Once you have that running, I recommend you try and make some tests in your own applications along the same sort of lines. While we will have sample code to play with for many chapters, I strongly suggest you try to test your own API (brand new or existing) too, as this is the most value you could get from the book.

Test. TEST. TEST YOUR APPLICATIONS.

Test Driven Development

Writing tests first is also a great way to go. Now that you have an understanding of your action plan, what the endpoints *should* be, and what their output *should* look like, you *should* be fine to build out tests against them even if they do not exist.

Running the tests will show you that everything is broken of course, so you'll just go through and build and test the endpoints one at a time. This sounds hard, but you just CANNOT afford to mess about with testing on an API.

Doing this first will save you a shit-ton of hard work down the road. I have the scars to prove it.

6. Outputting Data

6.1 Introduction

In Chapter 3: Input and Output Theory we looked at the theory of the output structure and the pros and cons for various different formats. The rest of this book assumes you have picked your favourite, and it assumes that favourite is my favourite. This does not matter all that much, but doing everything for everyone would be an exercise in futility and boredom.

The aim of this chapter is to help you build out your controller endpoints. Assuming you have written tests for these endpoints before they exist, we can now fill up a few of those tests with green lights (instead of the omnishambles of errors and fails you are most likely facing).

This example shows a list of places:

```
1   {
2       "data": [
3           {
4               "id": 2,
5               "name": "Videology",
6               "lat": 40.713857,
7               "lon": -73.961936,
8               "created_at": "2013-04-02"
9           },
10          {
11              "id": 1,
12              "name": "Barcade",
13              "lat": 40.712017,
14              "lon": -73.950995,
15              "created_at": "2012-09-23"
16          }
17      ]
18  }
```

Here is just the one place:

```
1  {
2      "data": [
3          "id": 2,
4          "name": "Videology",
5          "lat": 40.713857,
6          "lon": -73.961936,
7          "created_at": "2013-04-02"
8      ]
9  }
```

6.2 The Direct Approach

The first thing that every developer tries to do is take their favourite ORM, ODM, DataMapper, or Query Builder, pull up a query, then wang that result directly into the output.

Dangerously bad example of passing data from the database directly as output

```php
1  <?php
2  class PlaceController extends ApiController
3  {
4      public function show($id)
5      {
6          return json_encode([
7              'data' => Place::find($id)->toArray(),
8          ]);
9      }
10
11     public function index()
12     {
13         return json_encode([
14             'data' => Place::all()->toArray(),
15         ]);
16     }
17 }
```

This is the absolute worst idea you could have for enough reasons for me to fill up a chapter on its own, but I will try to keep it to just a section.

ORMs in Controllers

Your controller should definitely not have this sort of ORM/-Query Builder logic scattered around the methods. This is done to keep the example to one class.

Performance: If you return "all" items, the API will be fine during development, but suck when you have a thousand records in that table... or a million.

Display: PHP's popular SQL extensions all type cast all data coming out of a query as a string. So if you have a MySQL "boolean" field (generally this is a tinyint(1) field with a value of 0 or 1) it will display in the JSON output as a string with a value of "0" or "1", which is lunacy. If you're using PostgreSQL, it is even worse. The value directly output by PHP's PostgreSQL driver is "f" or "t". Your mobile developers won't like it one bit, and anyone looking at your public API is going to immediately consider this an amateur API. You want true or false as an actual JSON boolean, not a numeric string or a char(1).

Security: Outputting all fields can lead to API clients (users of all sorts) being able to view your users passwords, see sensitive information like email addresses for businesses involved (venues, partners, events, etc.), gain access to secret keys and tokens generally not allowed. If you leak your forgotten password tokens for example, then you're going to have an *extremely* bad time; it is as bad as leaking the password itself.

Some ORM's have a "hidden" option to hide specific fields from being output. If you can promise that you and every single other developer on your team (now, next year and for the entire lifetime of this application) will remember about that, then congratulations, you could also achieve world peace with a team that focused.

Stability: If you change the name of a database field, or modify your MongoDB document, or change the statuses available for a field between v3 and v4, then your API will continue to behave perfectly, but all of your iPhone users are going to have busted crashing applications — and it is your fault. You will promise yourself that you will avoid changing things, but you absolutely will. Change happens.

So, next, our theoretical developer friend will try hardcoding the output.

Laborious example of type casting and formatting data for output

```php
1   <?php
2   class PlaceController extends ApiController
3   {
4       public function show($id)
5       {
6           $place = Place::find($id);
7
8           return json_encode([
9               'data' => [
10                  'id'         => (int) $place->id,
11                  'name'       => $place->name,
12                  'lat'        => (float) $place->lat,
13                  'lon'        => (float) $place->lon,
14                  'created_at' => (string) $place->created_at,
15              ],
16          ]);
17      }
18
19      public function index()
20      {
21          $places = [];
22
23          foreach (Place::all() as $place) {
24              $places[] = [
25                  'id'         => (int) $place->id,
26                  'name'       => $place->name,
27                  'lat'        => (float) $place->lat,
28                  'lon'        => (float) $place->lon,
29                  'created_at' => (string) $place->created_at,
30              ];
31          }
32
33          return json_encode([
34              'data' => $places,
35          ]);
36      }
37  }
```

Thanks to specifying exactly what fields to return in the JSON array, the security issues are taken care of. The type casting of various fields turn numeric strings into integers, coordinates into floats, and that pesky Carbon (DateTime) object from Laravel into a string, instead of letting the object turn itself into an array.

The only issue this has not taken care of from the above example is performance, but that is a job for pagination, which will be covered in Chapter 10: Pagination.

A new issue has, however, been created. It should be a fairly obvious one; this is icky. Our theoretical developer now tries something else.

Considerably better approach to formatting data for output

```php
<?php
class PlaceController extends ApiController
{
    public function show($id)
    {
        $place = Place::find($id);

        return json_encode([
            'data' => $this->transformPlaceToJson($place),
        ]);
    }

    public function index()
    {
        $places = [];
        foreach (Place::all() as $place) {
            $places[] = $this->transformPlaceToJson($place);
        }

        return json_encode([
            'data' => $places,
        ]);
    }

    private function transformPlaceToJson(Place $place)
    {
        return [
            'id'        => (int) $place->id,
            'name'      => $place->name,
            'lat'       => (float) $place->lat,
```

```
31              'lon'        => (float) $place->lon,
32              'created_at' => (string) $place->created_at,
33          ];
34      }
35  }
```

Certainly much better, but what if a different controller wants to show a place at any point? You could theoretically move all of these transform methods to a new class or shove them in the ApiController, but that would just be odd.

Really, you want to make (what I have come to call) "transformers", partially because the name is awesome and because that is what they are doing — transforming data from the format it was stored as in the data store into something ready to be converted into JSON, or whatever else, with a bit more structure than just dumping out whatever your DB driver happened to give you.

I built a component to do this called Fractal[1], because PHP did not seem to have anything that would let me do this. Other languages have great solutions for this already. Some call it "data marshaling" or "serialization", but it is all achieving roughly the same goal: take potentially complicated data from a range of stores and turn it into a consistent output.

- Marshmallow[2] – Python
- ActiveModel Serializers[3] – Built for Rails API, which will be part of Rails 4.2
- Roar[4] – Ruby, but not limited to Rails or ActiveModel

6.3 Transformations with Fractal

With Fractal, transformers are created as either a callback, or an instance of an object implementing TransformerAbstract. They do exactly the job that our transformPlaceToJson() method did, but they live on their own,

---

[1]http://fractal.thephpleague.com/
[2]http://marshmallow.readthedocs.org/
[3]https://github.com/rails-api/active_model_serializers
[4]https://github.com/apotonick/roar

are easily unit testable (if that floats your boat), and remove a lot of presentation clutter from the controller.

Fractal does a lot more than that, which will be explored later on, but it covers concerns with transformation perfectly, removes the security, stability, and display concerns addressed earlier.

That is the end of theory in this book. We will now be working with code. Open up the Sample Code ZIP file, or head to the GitHub repo[5], and extract it somewhere useful.

```
1  $ cd chapter6
2  $ composer install
3  $ php artisan serve
4  Laravel development server started on http://localhost:8000
```

Open your browser and go to http://localhost:8000/places. There you'll see a list of places looking like this:

---

[5]https://github.com/philsturgeon/build-apis-you-wont-hate

```
{
  - embeds: [
        "checkins"
    ],
  - data: [
      - {
            id: 1,
            name: "Mireille Rodriguez",
            lat: -84.147236,
            lon: 49.254065,
            address1: "12106 Omari Wells Apt. 801",
            address2: "",
            city: "East Romanberg",
            state: "VT",
            zip: 20129,
            website: "http://www.torpdibbert.com/",
            phone: "(029)331-0729x4259"
        },
      - {
            id: 2,
            name: "Dr. Judd Goodwin",
            lat: -5.56932,
            lon: -50.95633,
            address1: "9060 Harvey Lodge Suite 527",
            address2: "",
            city: "New Lea",
            state: "AK",
            zip: 18211,
            website: "http://emard.com/",
            phone: "(193)893-3463x099"
        },
```

Fractal default JSON structure using the JSONView extension for Chrome

This is a Laravel application, but only because it has migrations and seeding and I like it. This is made up of a few bits of PHP that would work in any framework, and the approach works in any language.

- **composer.json** – Added an autoloadable folder using PSR-0 allowing my own code to be loaded
- **app/controllers/ApiController.php** – Insanely simple base controller for wrapping responses
- **app/controllers/PlaceController.php** – Grab some data and pass it to the `ApiController`

Other than defining some basic GET routes in `app/routes.php` that is basically all that is being done.

The `PlaceController` looks like this:

Example of a controller using Fractal to output data

```php
<?php
use App\Transformer\PlaceTransformer;

class PlaceController extends ApiController
{
    public function index()
    {
        $places = Place::take(10)->get();
        return $this->respondWithCollection($places, new PlaceTransformer);
    }

    public function show($id)
    {
        $place = Place::find($id);
        return $this->respondWithItem($place, new PlaceTransformer);
    }
}
```

The "raw data" (happens to be an ORM model but could be anything) is sent back with the appropriate convenience method, and a transformer instance is provided too. These `respondWithCollection()` and `respondWith-Item()` methods come from `ApiController` and their job is just to create Fractal instances without exposing as many classes to interact with.

The `PlaceTransformer` looks like this:

```php
<?php namespace App\Transformer;

use Place;
use League\Fractal\TransformerAbstract;

class PlaceTransformer extends TransformerAbstract
{
    /**
     * Turn this item object into a generic array
     *
```

```
11        * @return array
12        */
13       public function transform(Place $place)
14       {
15           return [
16               'id'           => (int) $place->id,
17               'name'         => $place->name,
18               'lat'          => (float) $place->lat,
19               'lon'          => (float) $place->lon,
20               'address1'     => $place->address1,
21               'address2'     => $place->address2,
22               'city'         => $place->city,
23               'state'        => $place->state,
24               'zip'          => $place->zip,
25               'website'      => $place->website,
26               'phone'        => $place->phone,
27           ];
28       }
29   }
```

Simple.

The ApiController is kept super simple at this point too:

Simple ApiController for basic responses using Fractal

```
1    <?php
2
3    use League\Fractal\Resource\Collection;
4    use League\Fractal\Resource\Item;
5    use League\Fractal\Manager;
6    use Illuminate\Routing\Controller;
7
8    class ApiController extends Controller
9    {
10       protected $statusCode = 200;
11
12       public function __construct(Manager $fractal)
13       {
14           $this->fractal = $fractal;
15       }
16
17       public function getStatusCode()
```

```
18      {
19          return $this->statusCode;
20      }
21
22      public function setStatusCode($statusCode)
23      {
24          $this->statusCode = $statusCode;
25          return $this;
26      }
27
28      protected function respondWithItem($item, $callback)
29      {
30          $resource = new Item($item, $callback);
31
32          $rootScope = $this->fractal->createData($resource);
33
34          return $this->respondWithArray($rootScope->toArray());
35      }
36
37      protected function respondWithCollection($collection, $callback)
38      {
39          $resource = new Collection($collection, $callback);
40
41          $rootScope = $this->fractal->createData($resource);
42
43          return $this->respondWithArray($rootScope->toArray());
44      }
45
46      protected function respondWithArray(array $array, array $headers = [])
47      {
48          return Response::json($array, $this->statusCode, $headers);
49      }
50
51  }
```

The method `respondWithArray()` takes a general array to convert into JSON, which will prove useful with errors. Other than that, everything you return will be a Fractal Item, or a Collection.

6.4 Hiding Schema Updates

Schema updates happen and they can be hard to avoid. If the change in question is simply a renamed field, then this is insanely easy to handle:

Before

```
1          'website' => $place->website,
```

After

```
1          'website' => $place->url,
```

By changing the right (our internal data structure) and keeping the left the same (the external field name), we maintain control over the outside stability for the client applications.

Sometimes it is a status change, a new status being added, or the change is fairly drastic and the statuses all change, but the old API version is still expecting the old ones. Maybe someone changed "available" to "active" to be consistent with the other tables because the original developer was as consistent and logical as a rabid ferret.

Before

```
1          'status' => $place->status,
```

After

```
1          'status' => $place->status === 'available' ? 'active' : $place->status,
```

Gross, but useful.

6.5 Outputting Errors

Exactly how to output errors is something I am still toying with myself. The current front runner is adding convenience methods to the `ApiController`, which handle global routes with a constant as the code and an HTTP error code set with an optional message in case I want to override the message.

Simple error codes and responses added to ApiController

```php
1   <?php
2
3   // ...
4
5   class ApiController extends Controller
6   {
7       // ...
8
9       const CODE_WRONG_ARGS = 'GEN-FUBARGS';
10      const CODE_NOT_FOUND = 'GEN-LIKETHEWIND';
11      const CODE_INTERNAL_ERROR = 'GEN-AAAGGH';
12      const CODE_UNAUTHORIZED = 'GEN-MAYBGTFO';
13      const CODE_FORBIDDEN = 'GEN-GTFO';
14
15      // ...
16
17      protected function respondWithError($message, $errorCode)
18      {
19          if ($this->statusCode === 200) {
20              trigger_error(
21                  "You better have a really good reason for erroring on a 200...",
22                  E_USER_WARNING
23              );
24          }
25
26          return $this->respondWithArray([
27              'error' => [
28                  'code' => $errorCode,
29                  'http_code' => $this->statusCode,
30                  'message' => $message,
31              ]
32          ]);
33      }
34
35      /**
36       * Generates a Response with a 403 HTTP header and a given message.
37       *
38       * @return  Response
39       */
40      public function errorForbidden($message = 'Forbidden')
41      {
```

```
42          return $this->setStatusCode(403)
43              ->respondWithError($message, self::CODE_FORBIDDEN);
44      }
45
46      /**
47       * Generates a Response with a 500 HTTP header and a given message.
48       *
49       * @return  Response
50       */
51      public function errorInternalError($message = 'Internal Error')
52      {
53          return $this->setStatusCode(500)
54              ->respondWithError($message, self::CODE_INTERNAL_ERROR);
55      }
56
57      /**
58       * Generates a Response with a 404 HTTP header and a given message.
59       *
60       * @return  Response
61       */
62      public function errorNotFound($message = 'Resource Not Found')
63      {
64          return $this->setStatusCode(404)
65              ->respondWithError($message, self::CODE_NOT_FOUND);
66      }
67
68      /**
69       * Generates a Response with a 401 HTTP header and a given message.
70       *
71       * @return  Response
72       */
73      public function errorUnauthorized($message = 'Unauthorized')
74      {
75          return $this->setStatusCode(401)
76              ->respondWithError($message, self::CODE_UNAUTHORIZED);
77      }
78
79      /**
80       * Generates a Response with a 400 HTTP header and a given message.
81       *
82       * @return  Response
83       */
84      public function errorWrongArgs($message = 'Wrong Arguments')
```

```
85        {
86            return $this->setStatusCode(400)
87                ->respondWithError($message, self::CODE_WRONG_ARGS);
88        }
89    }
```

This basically allows for generic error messages to be returned in your controller without having to think too much about the specifics.

Controller using Fractal, combined with a simple error response

```php
1    <?php
2    use App\Transformer\PlaceTransformer;
3
4    class PlaceController extends ApiController
5    {
6        public function index()
7        {
8            $places = Place::take(10)->get();
9            return $this->respondWithCollection($places, new PlaceTransformer);
10        }
11
12        public function show($id)
13        {
14            $place = Place::find($id);
15
16            if (! $place) {
17                return $this->errorNotFound(
18                    'Did you just invent an ID and try loading a place?'
19                );
20            }
21
22            return $this->respondWithItem($place, new PlaceTransformer);
23        }
24    }
```

Other "Place" specific errors could go directly into the PlaceController as methods just like these, with their own constants in the controller, picking a statusCode in the method, or relying on one as an argument.

6.6 Testing this Output

You have already seen how to test your endpoints using the Gherkin syntax in Chapter 5: Endpoint Testing, so we can apply that testing logic to this output:

```
1   Feature: Places
2
3   Scenario: Listing places without search criteria is not possible
4       When I request "GET /places"
5       Then I get a "400" response
6
7   Scenario: Finding a specific place
8       When I request "GET /places/1"
9       Then I get a "200" response
10      And scope into the "data" property
11          And the properties exist:
12              """
13              id
14              name
15              lat
16              lon
17              address1
18              address2
19              city
20              state
21              zip
22              website
23              phone
24              created_at
25              """
26          And the "id" property is an integer
27
28  Scenario: Searching non-existent place
29      When I request "GET /places?q=c800e42c377881f8ae509cf9a516d4eb59&lat=1&lon=1"
30      Then I get a "200" response
31      And the "data" property contains 0 items
32
33
34  Scenario: Searching places with filters
35      When I request "GET /places?lat=40.76855&lon=-73.9945&q=cheese"
36      Then I get a "200" response
```

```
37       And the "data" property is an array
38       And scope into the first "data" property
39           And the properties exist:
40               """
41               id
42               name
43               lat
44               lon
45               address1
46               address2
47               city
48               state
49               zip
50               website
51               phone
52               created_at
53               """
54       And reset scope
```

This is again using the `FeatureContext.php` provided in the sample code, which makes it really easy to test output. We are again assuming that all output is in a `"data"` element, which is either an object (when one resource has been requested), or an array of objects (multiple resources or a collection have been requested).

When you are searching for data, you want to ensure that a query not finding any data does not explode. This can be down to your controller processing on output and failing because what should be an `array` is `null`, or because some PHP collection class is missing methods, etc. This is why we perform the search with a hardcoded invalid search term and then check that it returns an empty collection:

```
1   {
2       "data": []
3   }
```

The line `And the "data" property contains 0 items` will cover this. Then we can search for valid terms, knowing that our database seeder has made sure at least one Place has the keyword "cheese" in the name. Using the line `And scope into the first "data" property` the scope changes to be inside the first data item returned, and the properties can be checked for existence too. If no data, or required fields are missing, this test will fail.

6.7 Homework

Your homework is to take apart the sample application, fit it into your API, and try to build valid output for as many of your GET endpoints as possible. Check the data types and make sure the array structure is output in the expected fashion using the test example above.

With valid output covered and basic errors covered, what is next? The most complicated part of API generation, which at some point every developer has to try and work out: embedding/nesting resources, or making "relationships".

7. Data Relationships

7.1 Introduction

If you have ever worked with relational databases, the chances are you understand relationships. Users have comments. Authors have one or many books. Books belong to a publisher. Southerners have one or more teeth. Whatever the example, relationships are incredibly important to any application and therefore an API too.

Relationships for your API output do not need to be directly mapped to database relationships. If your database relationships are built properly, relationships will often be similar, but your output might have extra dynamic relationships that are not defined by a JOIN, and might not necessarily include every possible database relationship.

Put more eloquently:

> REST components communicate by transferring a representation of a resource in a format matching one of an evolving set of standard data types, selected dynamically based on the capabilities or desires of the recipient and the nature of the resource. Whether the representation is in the same format as the raw source, or is derived from the source, remains hidden behind the interface. – Roy Fielding[1]

This explanation highlights an important factor: the output has to be based on the "desires of the recipient". There are many popular approaches to designing relationships, but many of them do not satisfy the "desires of the recipient". Still, I will cover the popular approaches with their pros and cons.

---

[1]http://www.ics.uci.edu/~fielding/pubs/dissertation/rest_arch_style.htm#sec_5_2

7.2 Subresources

One very simplistic way to approach related data is to offer up new URLs for your API consumers to digest. This was covered lightly in Chapter 2: Planning and Creating Endpoints and is a perfectly valid approach.

If an API has `places` as a resource and wants to allow access to a places check-ins, an endpoint could be made to handle exactly that:

/places/X/checkins

The downside here is that if you have already requested GET /places/X, then fetching the check-ins will require an extra HTTP request. Imagine a mobile app that wants to get all `places` in an area and put them on a map, then allow a user to browse through them. If the `place` search happens as one request, then the /places/X/checkins is executed each time the user clicks on a place, forcing the user to do a lot of unnecessary waiting. This is known as 1 + n, meaning the work done is increased by an extra one request for each `place` you look up.

That also assumes the only related data is check-ins. At Kapture, our API also had `merchant`, `images`, `current_campaign` and `previous_campaigns` to look up. Using "subresources" would only mean that four extra HTTP requests per place need to happen, which is 1 + 4n.

If 50 `places` were returned, and each time the related data had to be loaded, assuming the app user looked through all 50 `places`, there would be 1 initial request to get 50 results. Each of those results would require 4 more requests, meaning: 1 + (50 x 4) = 251. 251 HTTP requests happening (even assuming they are asyncronous) is just unnecessary, and going over HTTP on a mobile is the slowest things you can do. Even with caching, depending on the data set, it could still be 251 requests.

Some API developers try to avoid going over HTTP too many times by shoving as much data as possible into one request, so when you call the /places endpoint you automatically get `checkins`, `current_opps`, `merchants` and `images`. Unfortunately, shoving all of the information into the response (whether or not the client has indicated any interest in it) means waiting for huge file downloads full of irrelevant data! Even with GZIP compression enabled on the web server, downloading something you do not need is obviously not desirable, and can be avoided. This can mean major performance gains on mobile, and minor gains over a slow network, or weak Wi-Fi for desktop or tablets.

The trade-off here is between downloading enough data to avoid making the user wait for subsequent loads and downloading too much data to make them wait for the initial load is hard. An API needs the flexibility, and making subresources the only way to load related data is restrictive for the API consumer.

7.3 Foreign Key Arrays

Another approach to related data is to provide an array of foreign keys in the output. To use the JSON-API[2] standard as an example; if a post has multiple comments, the /posts endpoint might contain the following:

```
1  {
2    "post": {
3      "id": 1,
4      "title": "Progressive Enhancement is Dead",
5      "_links": {
6        "comments": ["1", "2"]
7      }
8    }
9  }
```

Here you still end up with n + 1 requests, but at least you can take those IDs and make a grouped request like /comments/1,2 or /comments?ids=1,2 to reduce how many HTTP requests are being made.

Back to the places example. If you have 50 places returned and need 4 extra pieces of data, you could iterate through the 50, map which items expect what pieces of data, request all unique pieces of data, and only end up with 1 + 4 = 5 HTTP requests instead of 251.

The downside is that the API consumer has to stitch all of that data together, which could be a lot of work for a large dataset.

---

[2]http://jsonapi.org/

7.4 Compound Documents (aka Sideloading)

Instead of just putting the foreign keys into the resource, you can take things a step further and sideload the data, which is also recommended by JSON-API.

> Compound documents contain multiple collections to allow for sideloading of related objects. Side-loading is desirable when nested representation of related objects would result in potentially expensive repetition. For example, given a list of 50 comments by only 3 authors, a nested representation would include 50 author objects where a sideloaded representation would contain only 3 author objects. – **Source:** canvas.instructure.com[3]

If we look at a collection of posts following the example from the section titled "Foreign Key Arrays," an API might show a response like this:

```
1   {
2     "posts": [{
3       "id": "1",
4       "title": "Awesome API Book",
5       "_links": {
6         "comments": ["1", "2"]
7       }, {
8       "id": "2",
9       "title": "But Really That API Book",
10      "_links": {
11        "comments": ["3"]
12      }
13    }],
14    "_linked": {
15      "comments": [
16        {
17          "id": "1"
18          "message": "Great book",
19          "created_at": "2014-08-23T18:20:03Z"
20        },
21        {
```

---

[3]https://canvas.instructure.com/doc/api/file.compound_documents.html

```
22          "id": "2"
23          "message": "I lolled",
24          "created_at": "2014-08-24T20:04:01Z"
25        },
26        {
27          "id": "3"
28          "message": "Ugh JSON-API...",
29          "created_at": "2014-08-29T14:01:13Z"
30        }
31      ]
32    }
33  }
```

Just like with the foreign key array approach, the client will have to do a lot of stitching together to map which comment belongs to which post. The data is all there, but getting it into a format for easy iteration could be a PITA.

That said, it will avoid duplicating the same item multiple times. While a comment would likely only be on a single post, if you were to include user information, the same user could show up multiple times as a commenter if they are active, or even as a commenter *and* a post author.

7.5 Embedded Documents (aka Nesting)

Instead of flattening the entire response to top level collections and losing the obvious context of the data, embedding data leaves it in the structure a client would expect.

This approach was used for the last two versions of the API at Kapture, and I used it on a few other APIs. It offers the most flexibility for the API consumer; it can reduce HTTP requests or reduce download size depending on what the consumer wants.

An API consumer could call the endpoint with the following query string parameter:

```
1  /places?include=checkins,merchant
```

This would alert Fractal (if properly configured) to include the checkins for that place, and the merchant data in the response inside the place resource:

```
 1  {
 2      "data": [
 3          {
 4              "id": 2,
 5              "name": "Videology",
 6              "lat": 40.713857,
 7              "lon": -73.961936,
 8              "created_at": "2013-04-02",
 9              "checkins" : [
10                  // ...
11              ],
12              "merchant" : {
13                  // ...
14              }
15          },
16          {
17              "id": 1,
18              "name": "Barcade",
19              "lat": 40.712017,
20              "lon": -73.950995,
21              "created_at": "2012-09-23",
22              "checkins" : [
23                  // ...
24              ],
25              "merchant" : {
26                  // ...
27              }
28          }
29      ]
30  }
```

Some systems (like Facebook, or any API using Fractal) will let you nest those embeds with dot notation:

E.g: `/places?include=checkins,merchant,current_opp.images`

Embedding with Fractal

Picking back up from chapter 6, your transformer at this point is mainly just giving you a method to handle array conversion from your data source to a simple array. Fractal can, however, include resources and collections too. Continuing the theme of users, places, and check-ins, the `UserTransformer` might have a check-ins list to see a users check-in history.

UserTransformer using Fractal

```php
<?php namespace App\Transformer;

use User;

use League\Fractal\TransformerAbstract;

class UserTransformer extends TransformerAbstract
{
    protected $availableEmbeds = [
        'checkins'
    ];

    /**
     * Turn this item object into a generic array
     *
     * @return array
     */
    public function transform(User $user)
    {
        return [
            'id'          => (int) $user->id,
            'name'        => $user->name,
            'bio'         => $user->bio,
            'gender'      => $user->gender,
            'location'    => $user->location,
            'birthday'    => $user->birthday,
            'joined'      => (string) $user->created_at,
        ];
    }

    /**
     * Embed Checkins
     *
     * @return League\Fractal\Resource\Collection
     */
    public function embedCheckins(User $user)
    {
        $checkins = $user->checkins;
```

```
39
40          return $this->collection($checkins, new CheckinTransformer);
41      }
42 }
```

The `CheckinTransformer` can then accept a `user` and a `place`. There is no
benefit to requesting the user in this context, because we know that
already, but asking for the place would return information about the
location that is being checked into.

CheckinTransformer using Fractal

```php
1  <?php namespace App\Transformer;
2
3  use Checkin;
4  use League\Fractal\TransformerAbstract;
5
6  class CheckinTransformer extends TransformerAbstract
7  {
8      /**
9       * List of resources possible to embed via this processor
10      *
11      * @var array
12      */
13     protected $availableEmbeds = [
14         'place',
15         'user',
16     ];
17
18     /**
19      * Turn this item object into a generic array
20      *
21      * @return array
22      */
23     public function transform(Checkin $checkin)
24     {
25         return [
26             'id'          => (int) $checkin->id,
27             'created_at'  => (string) $checkin->created_at,
28         ];
29     }
30
```

```
31      /**
32       * Embed Place
33       *
34       * @return League\Fractal\Resource\Item
35       */
36      public function embedPlace(Checkin $checkin)
37      {
38          $place = $checkin->place;
39
40          return $this->item($place, new PlaceTransformer);
41      }
42
43      /**
44       * Embed User
45       *
46       * @return League\Fractal\Resource\Item
47       */
48      public function embedUser(Checkin $checkin)
49      {
50          $user = $checkin->user;
51
52          return $this->item($user, new UserTransformer);
53      }
54  }
```

These examples happen to be using the lazy loading functionality of an ORM for `$user->checkins` and `$checkin->place`, but there is no reason that eager loading could not also be used by inspecting the `$_GET['include']` list of requested scopes. Something like this can easily go in your controller constructor somewhere in the base controller, or *something*:

Example of user input dictating which Eloquent ORM (Laravel) relationships to eager load

```
1   $requestedEmbeds = Input::get('include'); // ['checkins', 'place'] or just ['place']
2
3   // Left is relationship names. Right is include names.
4   // Avoids exposing relationships and whatever not directly set
5   $possibleRelationships = [
6       'checkins' => 'checkins',
7       'venue' => 'place',
8   ];
9
```

```
10  // Check for potential ORM relationships, and convert from generic "include" names
11  $eagerLoad = array_keys(array_intersect($possibleRelationships, $requestedEmbeds));
12
13  $books = Book::with($eagerLoad)->get();
14
15  // do the usual fractal stuff
```

Having the following code somewhere in the `ApiController`, or in your bootstrap, will make this all work:

```
1   class ApiController
2   {
3       // ...
4
5       public function __construct(Manager $fractal)
6       {
7           $this->fractal = $fractal;
8
9           // Are we going to try and include data?
10          if (Input::get('include')) {
11            $this->fractal->parseIncludes(Input::get('include'));
12          }
13      }
14
15      // ...
16  }
```

That is how you would do things in Laravel at least.

Embedding with Rails

The Rails lot are big fans of their ActiveRecord package, and most suggest using it to embed data. The specific part is in the Serializaton::to_json Documentation[4].

To include associations, use `blog.to_json(:include => :posts)`.

---

[4]http://apidock.com/rails/ActiveRecord/Serialization/to_json

```
1   {
2     "id": 1, "name": "Konata Izumi", "age": 16,
3     "created_at": "2006/08/01", "awesome": true,
4     "posts": [{
5       "id": 1,
6       "author_id": 1,
7       "title": "Welcome to the weblog"
8     }, {
9       "id": 2,
10      author_id: 1,
11      "title": "So I was thinking"
12    }]
13  }
```

Second level and higher order associations work as well:

```
1   blog.to_json(:include => {
2     :posts => {
3       :include => {
4         :comments => {
5           :only => :body
6         }
7       },
8       :only => :title
9     }
10  })
```

A little more complicated, but you get more control over what is returned:

```
1   {
2     "id": 1,
3     "name": "Konata Izumi",
4     "age": 16,
5     "created_at": "2006/08/01",
6     "awesome": true,
7     "posts": [{
8       "comments": [{
9         "body": "1st post!"
10      }, {
11        "body": "Second!"
12      }],
```

```
13       "title": "Welcome to the weblog"
14     },
15     {
16       "comments": [{
17         "body": "Don't think too hard"
18       }],
19       "title": "So I was thinking"
20     }]
21   }
```

This will work well, assuming everything is represented as ActiveRecord, which who knows, it might be.

7.6 Summary

The most important thing here is that an API has *some* way to include related data. Regardless of whether sideloading or embedding is the approach used, it is important to pick one.

One area that may affect your decision is using a JavaScript framework like EmberJS. In theory, an API should not concern itself with implementation specific details such as which JavaScript framework is being used, but if that EmberJS platform is a requirement of the business, then picking a compatible data structure known to work with it might be key.

At the time of writing, EmberJS (or more specifically EmberData) requires a specific sideloading approach, which might cause a headache for other consumers of your API. This is changing over time as EmberJS leans more towards JSON-API, but until JSON-API settles on v1.0 final they cannot be expected to maintain perfect support for the adapter.

Fractal will make your decision less important since using Serializers[5] allows you to switch between the two types rather easily. Later on in the book, we will talk about looking at MIME types and responding with different data, so it would not be difficult to use different headers for different data structures i.e., one custom output maybe using the embedded approach, and one JSON-API with sideloaded data.

---

[5]http://fractal.thephpleague.com/serializers/

8. Debugging

8.1 Introduction

Debugging is the art of working out why something is broken, which can be pretty difficult in an API. In much of web development, you are simply looking at what is output to the page, overusing `var_dump()`, or checking the browsers console for JavaScript errors.

Working with an API, you are mostly just working with requests and responses, but you need to initiate these requests in a repeatable way, often with full control over all of the HTTP headers, body content, etc.

There are a few methods you can utilize for debugging:

- Command-line debugging
- Browser debugging
- Network debugging

8.2 Command-line Debugging

Debugging via the command-line by using tools like `curl` is a great option for some. They tout the benefits of being able to do it from inside a network firewall. Certainly this can be an option for debugging live servers, but for development purposes (which is what we are doing here), using `curl` is just a lot of commands to remember for no reason.

```
1   $ curl -X POST http://localhost/places/fg345d/checkins --data @payload.json
```

It is not the most complicated way to initiate a request, but it is not the easiest. You will need to update that `payload.json` every time, or have a bunch of JSON in the CLI, and that can be really messy with multi-line payloads.

The CLI is a pain in the backside when you have a lot of endpoints with lots of potential values. Please, if you take yourself, your API, or your job as a developer seriously, do not do this.

8.3 Browser Debugging

Working in the browser is a great way to do things, and developers are fairly used to it. Sadly, most browsers can only really handle GET and POST requests by default, and a RESTful API requires PUT, DELETE, PATCH, etc., too. A well built RESTful API will also require the use of HTTP headers, which can be difficult to manipulate in a browser, as they are built to handle all of that for you.

HTTP Clients

Called a "HTTP client" or "REST client" interchangeably, these bits of software help perfectly with the job this book sets out to achieve: building nontrivial APIs. They allow you to format your HTTP request through a convenient GUI, choosing the HTTP verb, adding headers, entering a body, etc., then present the HTTP response to you with formatting or in source view if you prefer. Many of these GUIs will let you save common requests or build "collections" much like a set of bookmarks, but for your endpoints, and with all the correct headers and values.

These clients exist for Windows, OS X and Linux, but one that has really stood out to me is the Chrome extension called Postman[1].

---
[1]http://getpostman.com/

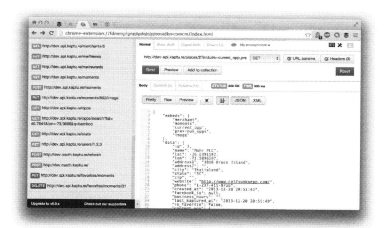

Postman HTTP Client, showing a collection and a successful JSON response

I have a collection, which almost mirrors my Behat tests, and have at least one for each endpoint, some with more.

Using Postman, I can develop "in the browser", see errors easily, keep changing things and click "send" for as long as I have to to make it work. When I expect it to work, I run the Behat scenario that covers the endpoint, and see if the tests are green. If Behat fails and the errors are not enough to resolve the problem, I then simply go back to Postman and try again.

Repeat until the endpoint "works" and passes the test.

Debug Panel

The approach above works fine if the problem is one that you can see. Anything to do with a slow page return, silent fails, unexpected results, etc., needs more information, and to do that you probably need another extension.

- **RailsPanel**[2] – Chrome-only DevTool panel with logging and profiling for Ruby on Rails (RailsCasts Video[3])

[2] https://github.com/dejan/rails_panel
[3] http://railscasts.com/episodes/402-better-errors-railspanel?view=asciicast

- **Clockwork**[4] – Chrome DevTool panel and standalone web app with logging and profiling for PHP
- **Chrome Logger**[5] – Chrome Logger only for Python, PHP, Ruby, Node, .NET, CF and Go

The first two are very similar and are the most feature filled, but the latter covers basic logging for a wider selection of languages.

Sure these examples are mostly Chrome, there are probably alternatives, but either way there is no harm in having Chrome as your development browser and continue to use your favourite for general browsing.

Clockwork showing the Laravel timeline in Chromium Browser

This timeline can be useful for working out where things are slowing down. Define your own events to see where the time is going.

Seeing logs in this panel is another benefit, and it helps keep you from switching back to the console all the time to catch the output of your logs via `tail -f`. Certainly you should be in the command line anyway, but constantly hitting `Alt+Tab` can cause distractions which slow you down.

---

[4]https://github.com/itsgoingd/clockwork-chrome
[5]http://craig.is/writing/chrome-logger

For those of you who normally debug with `var_dump()` or breakpoints, you could simply use Clockwork/RailsPanel/Chrome Logger to do it and see it in the panel, leaving your output untouched and avoiding tricky setup with IDE or other GUI programs.

CheckinTransformer using Fractal, with added Logging

```php
1   <?php namespace App\Transformer;
2
3   use Checkin;
4   use Log;
5
6   use League\Fractal\TransformerAbstract;
7
8   class CheckinTransformer extends TransformerAbstract
9   {
10      /**
11       * List of resources possible to embed via this processor
12       *
13       * @var array
14       */
15      protected $availableEmbeds = [
16          'place',
17          'user',
18      ];
19
20      /**
21       * Turn this item object into a generic array
22       *
23       * @return array
24       */
25      public function transform(Checkin $checkin)
26      {
27          return [
28              'id'         => (int) $checkin->id,
29              'created_at' => (string) $checkin->created_at,
30          ];
31      }
32
33      /**
34       * Embed Place
35       *
36       * @return League\Fractal\Resource\Item
```

```
37        */
38       public function embedPlace(Checkin $checkin)
39       {
40           $place = $checkin->place;
41
42           Log::info("Embedding place-{$place->id} into checkin-{$checkin->id}");
43
44           return $this->item($place, new PlaceTransformer);
45       }
46
47       /**
48        * Embed User
49        *
50        * @return League\Fractal\Resource\Item
51        */
52       public function embedUser(Checkin $checkin)
53       {
54           $user = $checkin->user;
55
56           Log::info("Embedding user-{$user->id} into checkin-{$checkin->id}");
57
58           return $this->item($user, new UserTransformer);
59       }
60   }
```

That will look a little something like this:

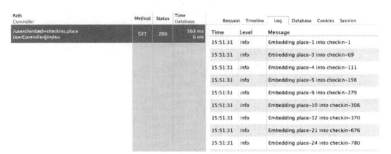

Clockwork showing the Log in Chromium Browser

You can log arrays and objects too:

Clockwork showing the Log in Chromium Browser

If logging something cannot help you with a problem, you need to log more things. Eventually you will work it out.

8.4 Network Debugging

The previously mentioned approaches to debugging are very much about being in control: create a request and see what happens with the response. Sometimes you need to debug what is happening to your API when the requests are not completely in control. If your iPhone developer comes over and says "the API is broken", it can be hard to work out why.

If you know exactly what endpoint is being hit and what the error is (because the iPhone dev is pointing to some debug data on his XCode screen), then maybe you can fix it, but often you will need more insight before you can recreate a bug. Maybe it is not even a request you can recreate easily (or at all), like anything to do with upload images as a PUT after getting them from the camera, or multiple requests that the iPhone app is executing in order using data from the previous requests.

Whatever the reason, sometimes you need to debug network activity to find out what is *actually* happening by spying on the request and getting the response.

Charles

If these are non-production errors that you want to debug against your local API and development iOS devices (aka the old iPhone you have not sold on eBay yet), then a great application is Charles[6].

---

[6]http://www.charlesproxy.com/

Charles essentially acts as an HTTP proxy, which means stuff comes in, stuff goes out, and Charles can show you what that was. Beyond that, it can rewrite headers and even let you modify the content of the request or response if you want.

To set the basics of this up, you first need to know the internal network of your machine.

Network Settings on Mac OS X, showing local IP

On your mobile device you will need to enable an HTTP Proxy. Enter your computer's local IP in the Proxy Server Address field, and select port 8888 – the default Charles port.

Sample Charles HTTP Proxy settings on iOS7

This will forward all web traffic to Charles, which (if it is running) will forward it on to its location.

As pointless as that might sound, the power comes in the options Charles has to offer. If we are intending to allow web traffic from our mobile device to the API on our development environment, at this point, we are half way.

Local vs. "Remote"

To allow Laravel (PHP's) built in server to access this connection on OS X, you must start the server using the network address shown in the sharing section of system preferences.
Choose Apple menu > System Preferences, and then click Sharing. Below "Computer Name" you will see an address followed by ".local".
To start the server simply use:

```
$ php artisan serve --host="Phils-MacBook-Air.local"
```

I personally have Charles pointing to a Vagrant box, running on its own IP address with its own virtual host enabled. This is not something that the book will cover, but is certainly something you should look into doing.

In order to make `dev-api.example.com` mean something on your mobile device, you need to enter a "Map Remote" rule in Charles.

Screenshot of Charles on OS X mapping dev–api.example.com

As explained above, Charles acts as a "man-in-the-middle", rerouting traffic based on your rules. By saying `dev-api.example.com` should be routed to `dev-api.example.com` on your machine, you have given that hostname, meaning on your mobile devices (or anything else talking to Charles on that port).

Now — so long as you are able to get a build of your mobile application pointing to `dev-api.example.com` — you will be able to click around the application, seeing requests and responses with all of the headers and values as you go.

Charles showing results for Kapture

You might not find yourself using Charles every day, or for a long time. At the start your HTTP Clients may be enough to debug problems, but having it available is certainly going to help you out at some point. Keep it in mind.

Wireshark[7] is also handy for Linux/OS X users, and Fiddler[8] is fun for Windows users.

[7]https://www.wireshark.org/
[8]http://www.telerik.com/fiddler

9. Authentication

9.1 Introduction

Understanding authentication for an API can be one of the largest hurdles for many developers, partially because there are a lot of different methods, but mostly because none of them are anything like authentication in an average web app.

When building an admin dashboard, CMS, blog, etc., it is widely accepted as standard behavior to use sessions with a data store such as cookies, Memcache, Redis, Mongo, or some SQL platform. Regardless of the data store, sessions are used so that once logged in, the browser remembers who the user is. To log in, the user is presented with a form in HTML showing two fields: one for the username and/or email address of the user, and one for the password. Once the end-user closes the browser or is inactive for a certain period of time, they will be forgotten.

This is the standard way to handle logins for the vast majority of sites built with a server-side language, but it is not how you handle authentication for an API at all.

In this chapter, we will look at some of the most popular authentication methods, and explain some pros and cons of each.

9.2 When is Authentication Useful?

Authentication allows APIs to track users, give endpoints user context ("find all of *my* posts"), limit users' access to various endpoints, filter data, or even throttle and deactivate accounts. This is all very useful for many APIs, but some may never need to implement authentication.

Read-only APIs

If your API is entirely read-only and the data is not sensitive, then you can just make it available and not worry about authentication. This is perfectly acceptable.

There is the concern that people could be attacking your API with DDoS attacks (flooding your API with an unreasonable number of requests with malicious intent). Using some form of authentication would limit the vectors of attack. To get a response from the API, they would need to be a valid user, and therefore the user's account could be throttled or deactivated if malicious activity was detected.

This does not entirely negate DDoS attacks, but it can help your API do less work as the request will terminate much sooner if an invalid user is found. So if DDoS issues are still a concern, with or without authentication, then use a self-improving firewall or implement other security barriers. Generally speaking, having anyone spamming any of your servers is not ideal, so this may certainly be a stronger move than implementing authentication purely to avoid these attacks.

Either way, you could quite easily release your API without authentication then implement piecemeal later on.

Internal APIs

If your API runs over a private network or is locked down with firewall rules and you do not require user context for your API, then you could probably skip authentication.

One concern with just leaving all the security up to the network is that, if the network is breached, then hackers would be able to do rather a lot of damage. However, if hackers are 'all up in your networks', then you probably have a lot of security issues already.

Keep it in mind.

9.3 Different Approaches to Authentication

Approach #1: Basic Authentication

The first approach that many developers go to is HTTP Basic, which is most like the standard username/password approach they have grown to know and love, but instead implemented on the HTTP Request level and respected by the browser.

Here is what Wikipedia has to say:

> HTTP Basic authentication (BA) implementation is the simplest technique for enforcing access controls to web resources because it doesn't require cookies, session identifier and login pages. Rather, HTTP Basic authentication uses static, standard HTTP headers which means that no handshakes have to be done in anticipation. – **Source:** Wikipedia[1]

Pros

- Easy to implement
- Easy to understand
- Works in the browser and any other HTTP client

Cons

- Is ludicrously insecure over HTTP
- Is fairly insecure over HTTPS
- Passwords can be stored by the browser, meaning a honeypot of user data is sitting around waiting to be gobbled up

Browsers Storing Passwords

With Chrome not even protecting these plain text passwords with a master password, you really are leaving your users wide open to attack if you let HTTP Basic be an option.

Elliott Kember publicly outed Chrome on this[2]. The Guardian cared[3]. Sir Tim Berners-Lee cared[4]. Google didn't[5].

---

[1] http://en.wikipedia.org/wiki/Basic_access_authentication
[2] http://blog.elliottkember.com/chromes-insane-password-security-strategy
[3] http://www.theguardian.com/technology/2013/aug/07/google-chrome-password-security-flaw?INTCMP=SRCH
[4] https://twitter.com/timberners_lee/status/364839351651274752
[5] https://news.ycombinator.com/item?id=6166886

More plain text Woe

Another security issue with Basic authentication is that it is ludicrously insecure when running over HTTP.

In the example provided by Wikipedia, a header will be placed in the HTTP request that looks like this:

> Authorization: Basic QWxhZGRpbjpvcGVuIHNlc2FtZQ==

If a request is made that goes over the wire (such as a JS based API request from a user sitting in a coffee shop), then that request could easily be intercepted. Taking that header as an example, it is insanely simple to find the username and password.

```
1  $ php -a
2  php > echo base64_decode('QWxhZGRpbjpvcGVuIHNlc2FtZQ==');
3  Aladdin:open sesame
```

This is no more or less secure than a HTML login form, but is certainly not secure enough for any API with sensitive data.

Using SSL improves the concerns greatly, but as the password is sent in every single HTTP request, there is still the potential for cracking it. At this point, though, somebody has to *really* want to get in.

HTTP Basic Auth may be a good fit for a relatively unimportant internal API, which needs some basic protection and needs to be implemented quickly, but certainly is not any good for anything that handles money, air traffic, or nuclear weapons.

Approach #2: Digest Authentication

Digest is an approach to authentication similar to Basic, but is designed to improve on the security concerns.

Instead of transmitting passwords in plain text, it will calculate a MD5 hash and send that. Unlike the Base64-based passwords used in the basic auth, MD5 is a one-way hash meaning you cannot simply take the hash and calculate the original password without trying out a lot of different combinations.

HA1 = MD5(A1) = MD5(username:realm:password) HA2 = MD5(A2) = MD5(method:digestURI) response = MD5(HA1:nonce:HA2)

The nonce is a unique number, which can contain (but should not be only) a timestamp. This helps to avoid replay attacks as the same hash will not be usable later on.

Pros

- Password is not transmitted in plain text
- The use of nonce helps negate rainbow table attacks
- Generally speaking, more secure than basic auth
- Easier to implement than some approaches

Cons

- Harder than basic auth to implement **well**
- Easy to implement badly
- Still insecure over HTTP
- Just like basic auth, passwords can still be stored by the browser
- Uses MD5

MD5… 4… 3… 2… 1… HACKED

MD5 is well accepted by many people today to be extremely crackable in most scenarios. Digest authentication has not improved since its creation in 1993. While the calculation process should help negate many of these issues, a lousy implementation of digest authentication will be open to some weird attack vectors that will remain unknown until after the fact.

Digest is certainly more secure than basic. It is great over SSL – definitely a good choice for an internal API if you have more time to spend implementing – but it still requires the username and password to be sent repeatedly, meaning it *is* potentially hackable if the hacker has enough encrypted requests available to process.

Approach #3: OAuth 1.0a

Not quite as popular these days, OAuth 1.0a was a big player on the web-based authentication scene and used by services such as Dropbox, Flickr, Twitter, Google, LinkedIn and Tumblr. Since then, most have moved over to OAuth 2, which we will discuss next. The two are very different beasts and should not be conflated.

> OAuth provides a method for clients to access server resources on behalf of a resource owner (such as a different client or an end-user). It also provides a process for end-users to authorize third-party access to their server resources without sharing their credentials (typically, a username and password pair), using user-agent redirections. – **Source:** Wikipedia[6]

Previously, we looked at authentication technologies that were essentially built into the browser, and were not particularly flexible in their usages. OAuth 1.0 was a great way for services such as social networks to implement web-based HTML login forms that looked the same as any other login form (were branded with logos, color schemes, etc) but could then send you back to the third party website for all sorts of awesome integration purposes.

For example, when Twitter swapped from HTTP Basic integration to OAuth 1.0 it meant that instead of third-parties (iPhone apps, other websites, CMSs, whatever) asking end-users to enter their username and password (which would be saved somewhere in plain text), the third party could redirect the user to the Twitter website, get them to log in, and have them come back to their service to save a special token, instead of saving a password. OAuth 1.0a called these tokens an 'OAuth Token' and an 'OAuth Token Secret'.

OAuth 1.0a was built to be very secure even when not running over SSL. That meant, of course, that it was incredibly complicated, having to set up signatures of which there were a few different algorithms, including HMAC-SHA1 and RSA-SHA1, or just plaintext. That got a bit tricky when trying to write client code, as you had to make sure you supported the right

---
[6]http://en.wikipedia.org/wiki/OAuth

signature algorithm, and most of the PHP implementations out there (including my old CodeIgniter library) did not support them all.

An average OAuth 1.0a signed HTTP request would look a little something like this:

```
1   POST /moments/1/gift HTTP/1.1
2   Host: api.example.com
3   Authorization: OAuth realm="http://sp.example.com/",
4   oauth_consumer_key="0685bd9184jfhq22",
5   oauth_token="ad180jjd733klru7",
6   oauth_signature_method="HMAC-SHA1",
7   oauth_signature="wOJIO9A2W5mFwDgiDvZbTSMK%2FPY%3D",
8   oauth_timestamp="137131200",
9   oauth_nonce="4572616e48616d6d65724c61686176",
10  oauth_version="1.0"
11  Content-Type: application/json
12
13  { "user_id" : 2 }
```

Ouch.

Another complication was that there were different implementations: two-legged ("proper" and "not proper") and three-legged. This is incredibly confusing, so I will let Mashape explain in the OAuth Bible: OAuth Flows[7].

There was also xAuth (which is still OAuth 1.0a), designed for mobile and desktop applications that do not have easy access to a browser. It is much easier for a web application to spawn a popup with JavaScript, or to redirect a user, than it is for a mobile app. This made it a much handier way to get OAuth Tokens than the other implementations.

In the end, if you got the OAuth Token and Secret, you would place the OAuth Token in the request as a header and use the secret to sign the signature, which would encrypt the request and make the whole thing nice and secure. If you can shove SSL on top of that, then you have got yourself a very secure setup - except for the fact that tokens would stay the same once created, so over time their security could be compromised.

---

[7]https://github.com/Mashape/mashape-oauth/blob/028860c/FLOWS.md#oauth-10a-one-legged

Somebody could recover the data from a laptop you sold them on eBay, or a potential hacker could packet sniff enough traffic signed with your signature to eventually programmatically guess the token and secret.

Pros

- Super secure, even without SSL
- Does not send username/password in every request (plain text or hashed)
- Stops third party applications wanting or storing your username and password
- An attacker gaining an OAuth Token and even a Secret should still never be able to change your password, meaning you should be safe from account hijack

Cons

- Rather complicated to interact with, even if you have a well built client library. PHP never really had one, but The League of Extraordinary Packages[8] has recently built a decent one[9]
- Limited number of ways to grant access. xAuth and Two/Three-legged flows ended up being rather restrictive
- Tokens never changed, so security was essentially just a matter of how long and how much you used the service

OAuth 1.0a would be a great technology to implement if you were building a website with a public user-based API... and you were building it in 2009-2010. Now, probably not.

Approach #4: OAuth 2.0

OAuth 2 dropped the secret token, so users are simply getting an *access token* now. It also dropped signature encryption. This was seen by many as a massive step backwards in security, but it was actually rather a wise move. The OAuth 1.0a spec made SSL optional, but OAuth 2.0 requires

---

[8]http://thephpleague.com/
[9]https://github.com/thephpleague/oauth1-client

it. Relying on SSL to handle the encryption of the request is logical and drastically improves the implementation.

Even a basic GET request in OAuth 1.0a was horrendous as you would always need to set up your consumers, signatures, etc., but with OAuth 2.0 you can simply do this:

```
1  file_get_contents('https://graph.facebook.com/me?access_token=vr5HmMkzlxKE70W1y4Mi');
```

Or, as we saw back in chapter 3, you can usually pass access tokens to the server as an HTTP request header:

```
1  POST /moments/1/gift HTTP/1.1
2  Host: api.example.com
3  Authorization: Bearer vr5HmMkzlxKE70W1y4Mi
4  Content-Type: application/json
5
6  { "user_id" : 2 }
```

That looks a little easier to work with than OAuth 1.0a, right?

Headers vs. URL

You should always try to use the `Authorization` header to send your tokens whenever possible. The query-string is secured when using SSL, but unless they are intentionally blocked then access tokens could start turning up in server logs and various other places. Also, browsers will store the full URL (including query-string) in history. This could easily compromise the integrity of users security if their computer is stolen or if a sibling decides to play a prank.

"Short"-life Tokens

As discussed, OAuth 1.0a also uses the same tokens essentially forever. OAuth 2.0's access tokens will (can) expire after an arbitrary period of time, which is defined by the OAuth server. When you request an access token, you will usually be provided with a *refresh token* and an *expiry offset*, which is the number of seconds until the token expires. Some servers send you a unix time at which it expires. Folks like to do things different for some reason, but if you know what to look out for it is not so bad.

Using the expire time you know when your access token will not be valid, so you can proactively create a CRON job that refreshes the access tokens, or you can wrap your HTTP requests in an exception handler that looks for a 'Not Authorized' error and then refreshes them as the OAuth 2.0 spec recommends.

This extra "access tokens expire and you have to refresh them" step initially seems confusing and annoying, especially when you are used to "once I have this token it works forever". However, it is much more secure. OAuth 1.0a stopped you handing out your username and password by essentially giving you another username and password (the token and the secret), which worked for one specific client. Any good network admin will tell you that you should regularly change your password (at least once every month), and OAuth is no different as the more you use the same password/token the greater your chance of somebody finding out what it is.

Grant Types

One further massive benefit OAuth 2.0 provides over OAuth 1.0a is the ability to have multiple (even custom) grant types. Grant types are essentially a "mode" in which the OAuth 2.0 server will run, expecting different inputs and maybe providing different outputs. With this flexibility, you can create some amazing implementations.

The most common OAuth 2.0 Grant Type that a user will be familiar with is `authorization_code`, which is a very OAuth 1.0a-like flow.

A client web app creates a link to the OAuth Server of the service they would like to log into (e.g. Facebook), and the user logs in. Facebook redirects the user back to the client web app's 'Callback URL' with a `?code=FOO` variable in the query string. The web app then takes that code and makes a second request to Facebook (usually a `POST`, but sometimes a `GET` depending on which popular API you look at) and Facebook then offers up an access token in the response. Some other popular APIs, like Google Apps, then provide `expires` and a refresh token too.

This is just one approach and there are more. Due to this flexibility, OAuth 2.0 is good for pretty much any scenario when authenticating an API, be it a basic username password login on a single-page JavaScript app, a CRON job that has no database access, or a full blown user-redirect flow between different websites. The flexibility of custom grant types allows absolutely anything to be done.

More on this in the 'Understanding OAuth 2.0 Grant Types' section below.

Erin Hammer

Often, I am asked why anyone would still use OAuth 2.0 after Erin Hammer (lead author and editor of the OAuth 2.0 standard) withdrew his name from the specification[10]. It certainly sent a ripple through the Internet, but I personally disagree wholeheartedly with the issues he raised.

1. OAuth 2.0 is less secure if you do not use SSL/TSL. Correct. So use them.
2. People have implemented OAuth 2.0 badly (looking at you Facebook/Google/most providers), but when implemented well it is lovely. Use a pre-built standard compliant implementation.
3. He thinks refresh tokens are annoying, but I think they are great.

His departure from the project is no major loss. I am sure the IETF are bikeshedding hard, but after using both for years, I am much happier with OAuth 2.0 and really wish Twitter would get on with a full upgrade[11] so I never have to use OAuth 1.0a again.

Generally speaking, OAuth 2.0 is a good fit for a huge majority of situations, provided you **use SSL** and implement a **well-tested** existing solution for your OAuth 2.0 Server. Trying to do this yourself can be incredibly hard and may well lead to you getting super-hacked. Even Facebook have trouble here to this day because they rolled their own solution based on a really early draft of the specification.

Other Approaches

- **OpenID** - https://openid.net/
- **Hawk** - https://github.com/hueniverse/hawk
- **Oz** - https://github.com/hueniverse/oz

---

[10]http://hueniverse.com/2012/07/26/oauth-2-0-and-the-road-to-hell/
[11]https://dev.twitter.com/discussions/397

9.4 Implementing an OAuth 2.0 Server

Implementation by hand of an OAuth 2.0 server - or any of these authentication methods for that matter - can be very difficult. This chapter,
aimed to explain the pros, cons, and use cases for each, and implementation, is sadly out of its scope. Here are a few existing implementations
that you could look into using.

PHP Implementations

One implementation stands out above the rest in PHP land, and not just
because it is written by a friend of mine, Alex Bilbie[12]. He has studied both
OAuth specs religiously and over the years has built some great tools for
them, which I have used many times.

In his last job at the University of Lincoln, he was using OAuth for all
sorts of cool things. He then received a huge amount of funding for
a research project to build awesome open-source code for improving
authentication and interoperability. That project resulted in a few great
packages, including the PHP OAuth 2.0 Server[13]. It has a bridge-package
for Laravel, which makes it trivial to implement.

There is another PHP OAuth 2.0 server implementation[14] that has been
around for roughly the same amount of time and is also of great quality.
The two approaches are a little different but both implement the full spec,
so have a click around and see which you prefer.

Python Implementations

There are two implementations for Python that look fairly good. One is
oauth2lib[15], which is a fork of pyoauth2[16]. The original authors gave up,
then the new ones had to rename it, or something like that.

---

[12] http://alexbilbie.com/
[13] http://oauth2.thephpleague.com/
[14] http://bshaffer.github.io/oauth2-server-php-docs/
[15] https://github.com/NateFerrero/oauth2lib
[16] https://github.com/StartTheShift/pyoauth2

Another is python-oauth2[17], which was developed by SimpleGeo, a great geo-location/place SaaS. This has since been bought out and shut down and was last committed to around two years ago. Maybe somebody needs to take that one over too.

Ruby Implementations

For an API I worked on after Kapture, we had a Rails codebase and implemented Doorkeeper[18] with great success. Doorkeeper supports the main grant types, has great documentation and is being actively developed by a very responsive team of contributors. It also documents some simple integration for Devise - a popular user / authentication system for Rails.

There is also a Rack module named Rack::OAuth2::Server[19]. I have no experience using it, but it seems actively developed and has documentation to implement into Rails, Sinatra and Padrino.

9.5 Where the OAuth 2.0 Server Lives

Many assume that the OAuth 2.0 server should be part of their API server. While it certainly could, it definitely does not need to be.

An OAuth server usually has a web interface, which has HTML forms, form validation, and all sorts of static resources like images, CSS, JavaScript, etc. That makes it more fitting with a general website. If your API and website are different servers, then the OAuth server would be more suitably placed on the website.

That said, it is better to keep all of these things seperate and autonomous, since if you decide to build a new version of your website in AngularJS instead of server-side code it would be a pain to have to switch your OAuth server implementation too. If the OAuth server is on its own server, or at very least its own code base, then you do not have this concern.

The only thing your API needs to do is look for an access token (as a header or query string parameter), then hit whichever data store (SQL database,

[17]https://github.com/simplegeo/python-oauth2
[18]https://github.com/doorkeeper-gem/doorkeeper
[19]https://github.com/assaf/rack-oauth2-server

Mongo, etc.) contains the access tokens. Check it is valid (in the DB and not expired), then grab whichever user is tied to it, and pull that record for use throughout the API code.

None of that is complicated, so trying to tie the API server and OAuth server together in the same application code base out of some misplaced perception of belonging is just not required.

9.6 Understanding OAuth 2.0 Grant Types

The four grant types discussed in the specification are:

Authorization Code

"Authorization code" is the full user flow with redirects discussed earlier in the chapter.

This is most useful if you have multiple sites (like a network of sites for games, movies, books, etc.), or just want to share logins with other partners. This is also the grant type you will most likely use to log users into Facebook or Google.

Section 4.1 in the spec[20]

Refresh Token

"Refresh tokens" are supported by most popular OAuth 2.0 providers. Basically, you notice that your old access token does not work anymore when you receive an HTTP 401 status code, so you request a new one using your refresh token. The OAuth 2.0 server will then either give you a new access token, or the server will refuse. At that point, you will have to send your user an email saying, "your account is no longer connected to Example.com, please click here to reconnect". This is not common, and usually means that the user has disconnected access for that account anyway, so a manual request is literally the only option.

This sounds like a bit of a runaround, but it is quite simple and has a few advantages.

---

[20]http://tools.ietf.org/html/rfc6749#section-4.1

Basically, if you are using the same access token over and over again forever then there is a fairly strong chance of somebody finding it. There are an array of reasons for this, from the site not implementing SSL, the site getting hacked, the sys admins accidentally exposing some of their access logs, or, more likely, the access token being stored in the browser.

Storing the access token in the browser is fine if the access token is going to expire soon, as it means the hacker has a very short window of opportunity to do anything if they find it. If they get the current access token then fine, but if there is a five minute expiry then getting that token would be much more difficult, and would probably require the hacker to be physically on the device you were using, or SSHing in – at which point you have much greater concerns.

Not all APIs will expire their access tokens, so some do live forever. Normally they either last forever, or they will give you an expiry time and expect you to refresh them. One exception to that is Facebook, who do neither. Facebook's whole approach is that they *want* you to be forced to send a user back to `facebook.com` on a login.

It is frustrating that once again Facebook have decided to flagrantly disregard the OAuth 2.0 spec to suit their own needs, hurting the user flow and confusing developers in the process. Working with these popular APIs you will notice a lot of things like this that wind you up, but the differences are much less problematic if they are not even slightly OAuth 2.0 based. At least they have *some* common ground.

Section 6 in the spec[21]

Client Credentials

Client credentials can be useful for saying:

> I am an application, you know that I am an application because here are my client_id and client_secret values. Let me in now please.

This is useful for CRON jobs, worker processes, daemons or any other sort of background process. The application will not have any context of

---

[21]http://tools.ietf.org/html/rfc6749#section-6

a user, but it will be able to interact with your API. They have an access token which they will keep on using, and if it happens to expire then the background process will know how to refresh it.

Twitter, as mentioned, have been OAuth 1.0a only for years, but they added an OAuth 2.0 endpoint which would accept `client_credentials` as the only grant type. Their documentation[22] explains further.

This is handy for public crawling of tags or public tweets, but is not able to handle posting statuses or anything that relates to a user. This is a handy compromise for now, and hopefully is a sign that they intend to roll out support for more grant types in the future.

Section 2.3.1 in the spec[23]

Password (user credentials)

User Credentials are possibly the easiest way to get an access token for a user. This skips the whole redirect flow that 'Authentication Code' provides, and the user peace-of-mind that comes with it, but does offer simplicity. If Twitter had offered User Credentials OAuth 2.0 login as a replacement for HTTP Basic, then the 'Twitter Authpocolypse' a few years ago would have been far less drastic.

All you need to do is provide a username and password to the OAuth 2.0 server, and it gives you back an access token (and of course maybe a refresh token). Simple.

An example of this being extremely useful is creating a single page application with AngularJS/EmberJS/WhateverJS and wanting to provide a login. Clearly redirecting users around would be unnecessary because they are already on "your site", and the login box can be already styled however you like.

The trouble is, if you try to do all of this in JavaScript code, you run into a problem. You need to send the `client_id` and `client_secret` along with the `username` and `password`, but if you are using JavaScript then putting your `client_secret` into the JavaScript means it is readable in the browser.

HACK HACK HACK!

---

[22]https://dev.twitter.com/docs/auth/application-only-auth
[23]http://tools.ietf.org/html/rfc6749#section-2.3.1

Do not do that.

It is easily avoidable; simply make a proxy script that will take a username and password as POST items, then pass them onto the OAuth 2.0 server with the `client_id` and `client_secret` too, both of which probably come from some secret config file on the server.

Basic access token proxy script written in Python using Flask

```python
1   import requests
2
3   from flask import Flask
4
5   app = Flask(__name__)
6
7   @app.route('/proxy/access_token', methods=['POST'])
8   def access_token():
9
10      payload = {
11          'grant_type': 'password',
12          'client_id': 'foo',
13          'client_secret': 'bar',
14          'username': request.form['username'],
15          'password': request.form['password']
16      }
17
18      r = requests.post('https://oauth.example.com/', data=payload)
19
20      return r.json(), r.status_code
```

That is all that needs to be done. Take whatever it gives you, pass it onto the server, and pass the response back. This keeps the secret information secret and still lets you do everything else in the browser.

Section 4.3 in the spec[24]

Custom Grant Types

At Kapture, we created a `social` grant, where a user would provide a string matching `"facebook"` or `"twitter"` and an `access_token` (with maybe a

[24]http://tools.ietf.org/html/rfc6749#section-4.3

`access_token_secret` for OAuth 1.0a providers like Twitter) and that would do the following:

1. Grab the user's data
2. Find out if they are a Kapture user, and if not create a Kapture user record
3. Create an access token, refresh token, etc. to give that user access

That gave us a completely seamless instant sign-up or log in experience for our iPhone application, and let our admin panel AND merchant dashboard use the exact same OAuth 2.0 server to handle logins for everyone. Very handy for our iPhone app and meant that we could roll the same functionality out to a potential Android app and web-based versions too.

If you can think of it, you can make a custom grant type for it. Grant access to any users that provide you with a URL of an image, which contains a photograph of a car which happens to be yellow. Whatever.

10. Pagination

10.1 Introduction

Pagination is one of those words that means something very specific to many developers, but it generally means:

> The sequence of numbers assigned to pages in a book or periodical.

There are a few ways to achieve pagination, but when talking in terms of an API it means:

> Any way you want to go about splitting up your data into multiple HTTP requests, for the sake of limiting HTTP Response size.

There are a few reasons for doing this:

1. Downloading more stuff takes longer
2. Your database might not be happy about trying to return 100,000 records in one go
3. Presentation logic iterating over 100,000 records is no fun

As you can probably tell, 100,000 is an arbitrary number. An API could have endpoints like /places with over a million records, or check-ins which could be unlimited. While developing an API, many people forget about this, and while ten or a hundred records will display quite quickly during development, infinity is considerably slower. Data grows exponentially.

A good API will allow the client to request the number of items it would like returned per HTTP request. Some developers try to be smart and use custom HTTP headers for this, but this is literally what the query string is for.

/places?number=12

Some use `number`, `limit`, `per_page` or whatever. I always think `limit` only really makes sense because SQL users are used to it and an API is not SQL, so personally I use `number`.

 Define a Maximum

When you take the limit/number parameter from the client, you absolutely have to set an upper bound on that number, make sure it is over 0 and depending on the data source you might want to make sure it is an integer as decimal places could have some interesting effects.

10.2 Paginators

I stole the word "paginator" from Laravel, which uses a `Paginator` class for a very specific type of pagination. It is not the most efficient form of pagination by any means, but it is rather easy to understand and works fine on relatively small data sets.

How do Paginators Work

One approach to pagination is to count how many records there are for a specific item. So, if we count how many `places` there are, there will probably be some sort of SQL query like this:

```
1   SELECT count(*) as `total` FROM `places`
```

When the answer to that query comes back as `1000`, the following code will be executed:

```php
1   <?php
2   $total = count_all_the_places();
3   $page = isset($_GET['page']) ? (int) $_GET['page'] : 1;
4   $per_page = isset($_GET['number']) ? (int) $_GET['number'] : 20;
5   $page_count = ceil($total / $per_page);
```

With that basic maths taken care of, we know how many pages there are in total, and have rounded it up with `ceil()`. This is a PHP function equivalent of `Math.round()`, which rounds it up to the nearest integer. If `$total` is 1000, then `$page_count` will be 83.333. Obviously nobody wants to go to page 83.333, so round that up to page 84.

Using these variables, an API can output some simple metadata that goes next to the main `data` namespace:

```json
1   {
2       "data":[
3           ...
4       ],
5       "pagination":{
6           "total":1000,
7           "count":12,
8           "per_page":12,
9           "current_page":1,
10          "total_pages":84,
11          "next_url":"/places?page=2&number=12"
12      }
13  }
```

The names of items in this pagination example are purely based on what Kapture's iPhone developer suggested at the time, but should portray the intent.

You basically give the client enough information to do maths itself, if that is something it wants to do, or you let them ingest basic HTTP links too.

Counting lots of Data is Hard

The main trouble with this method is the SELECT count(*) that is required to find out the total, which can be a very expensive request.

The first thing to mind will be caching. Sure, you can cache the count, or even prepopulate the request. In many cases you certainly could, but you have to consider that most endpoints will have multiple query string parameters to customise the data returned.

/places?merchant=X

That means you will now have a single cache for every count of places by each specific merchant. That could also be cached or prepopulated, but when it comes to geo data you have no chance:

/places?lat=42.2345&lon=1.234

Unfortuntately, the chances of having multiple people request the exact same set of coordinates regularly enough to make a cache worthwhile is unlikely, especially as those coordinates point to a remote, mountainous region of Spain.

Prepopulation for those results also seems highly unlikely. If you have literally millions of places then trying to count all places for somebody in Spain is just silly. Indexes can help. Slicing your data into geographic buckets and pulling it together with some clever trickery can help. Generally speaking though, using this sort of pagination introduces big data problems to what can be potentially small data setups, especially when you have filtering options.

This is not bad (and I have used it myself for plenty of APIs), but you definitely need to keep this sort of thing in mind.

Moving Goal Posts

Another tricky issue with the count-everything-then-pick-which-page-number approach is that if a new item is added between HTTP requests, the same content can show up twice.

Imagine the scenario, where the `number` per page is set to 2, `places` are ordered by name, and the values are hip bars in Brooklyn, NY:

- Page 1

- Barcade
- Pickle Shack
- Page 2
  - Videology

If the client requests Page 1, then they will see the first two results. While the results for Page 1 are being displayed to the end user, some hip new bar opens up with the name "Lucky Dog" and joins the platform.

Now the data set looks like this:

- Page 1
  - Barcade
  - Lucky Dog
- Page 2
  - Pickle Shack
  - Videology

If the client does not refresh Page 1 (which most would not do for the sake of speed) then "Pickle Shack" is going to show up twice, and "Lucky Dog" will not be on the list at all.

Using Paginators with Fractal

This is a rather specific example, requiring Laravel's Eloquent and Pagination packages, and Fractal[1]. If you are not using any of those things then you can skip it and just use some simple maths like the example JSON above. Otherwise, follow on:

---

[1]http://fractal.thephpleague.com/

```php
<?php
use Acme\Model\Place;
use Acme\Transformer\PlaceTransformer;
use League\Fractal\Resource\Collection;
use League\Fractal\Pagination\IlluminatePaginatorAdapter;

$paginator = Place::findNearbyPlaces($lat, $lon)->paginate();
$places = $paginator->getCollection();

$resource = new Collection($places, new PlaceTransformer);
$resource->setPaginator(new IlluminatePaginatorAdapter($paginator));
```

10.3 Offsets and Cursors

Another common pagination method the use of "cursors", sometimes called "markers". A cursor is usually a unique identifier, or an offset, so that the API can just request more data.

If there is more data to be found, the API will return that data. If there is not more data, then either an error (404) or an empty collection will be returned.

Empty is not Missing

I personally advise against a 404 because the URL is not technically wrong, there is simply no data to be returned in the collection so an empty collection makes more sense.

To try the same example:

```json
{
    "data":[
        ...
    ],
    "pagination":{
        "cursors":{
            "after":12,
            "next_url":"/places?cursor=12&number=12"
        }
    }
}
```

This JSON has been returned `after` requesting the first 12 records. 1-12 were all available and, for the sake of example, were all auto-increment integers. Therefore, in this example, if we would like the content that is *after* 12, then the records having ID from 13 to 24 would be on the next page.

While this provides a very simplified explanation, generally speaking using IDs is a tricky idea. A specific record can move from one category to another, or could be deactivated, or all sorts of things. You *can* use IDs, but it is generally considered best practice to use an offset instead.

Using an offset is simple. Regardless of your IDs — auto-incrementing, UUID, etc. — you simply put 12 in there and say "I would like 12 records, with an offset of 12", instead of saying "I would like records after id=12".

Obscuring Cursors

Facebook sometimes use cursors to obscure actual IDs, but sometimes use them for "cursor based offsets". Regardless of what the cursor actually is, your user should never really care, so obfuscating it seems like a good idea.

```
        }
    ],
    "paging": {
        "cursors": {
            "after": "NA==",
            "before": "MQ=="
        }
    }
}
```

Facebook Graph API using Cursors

How did Facebook get `"NQ="` and `"MQ=="` as values? Well, they are intentionally odd looking as you are not meant to know what they are. A cursor is an opaque value which you can pass to the pagination system to get more information, so it could be 1, 6, 10, 120332435 or Tuesday and it would not matter.

Don Gilbert[2] let me know that in the example of Facebook they just Base64 encode their cursors:

---

[2]http://dongilbert.net/

```
1  php > var_dump(base64_decode('NQ='));
2  string(2) "5"
3
4  php > var_dump(base64_decode('MQ=='));
5  string(1) "1"
```

Obfuscating the values is not done for security but, I assume, to avoid people trying to do maths on the values. Ignorance is bliss in this scenario, as somebody doing maths on an offset-based paginated result might end up using the same calculation on a primary key integer. If everything is an opaque cursor or marker then nobody can do that.

Extra Requests = Sadness

This approach is not favoured by some client developers, as they do not like the idea of having to make extra HTTP requests to find out that there is no data. However, this seems like the only realistic way to achieve a performant pagination system for large data. Even with a "pages" system, if there is only one record on the last page and that record (or any other in any page) is removed, then the last page will be empty anyway. Every pagination system needs to respond to an empty collection.

Using Cursors with Fractal

Again this is a rather specific example, but should portray the concept.

```
1  <?php
2  use Acme\Model\Place;
3  use Acme\Transformer\PlaceTransformer;
4  use League\Fractal\Cursor\Cursor;
5  use League\Fractal\Resource\Collection;
6
7  $current = isset($_GET['cursor']) ? (int) base64_decode($_GET['cursor']) : 0;
8  $per_page = isset($_GET['number']) ? (int) $_GET['number'] : 20;
9
10 $places = Place::findNearbyPlaces($lat, $lon)
11   ->limit($per_page)
12   ->skip($current)
13   ->get();
```

```
14
15   $next = base64_encode((string) ($current + $per_page));
16
17   $cursor = new Cursor($current, $next, $places->count());
18
19   $resource = new Collection($places, new PlaceTransformer);
20   $resource->setCursor($cursor);
```

This will take the current cursor, use it as an offset, then work out the base64 version and convert it. There is a bit of work to do in this example because the Cursor class is intentionally vague. Instead of using an offset it could be a specific ID and you use it for an SQL WHERE id > X clause, but better not.

Pagination with the Link Header

The Link header is one not often used, but was introduced in RFC 5988[3] for just this sort of thing.

Example showing GitHub's use of the Link header in an HTTP response

```
1   Link: <https://api.github.com/user/repos?page=3&per_page=100>; rel="next",
2   <https://api.github.com/user/repos?page=50&per_page=100>; rel="last"
```

I have never used this and am dubious. Some argue that pagination is metadata, and metadata should be kept out of the response.

Inserting pagination data into the API response in a 'pagination' namespace is very common and has been my go-to solution for years. I would slot it next to the 'data' namespace, and that makes it very easy for clients who a) cannot read those HTTP headers and b) do not know to look there.

That said, using the Link header can help you avoid the need to wrap your collections in a namespace at all. This might be something that interests you, as through developing Fractal I ran into many developers who *hate* using a namespace for their collections.

The final advantage to mention would be that the Link is standard. Parsing it is going to be 100% the same for each API, and will not expect the client to work out if the link is contained in uri, url, href or something else.

---

[3]http://tools.ietf.org/html/rfc5988#page-6

Every API should choose its approach to pagination itself. Using this specific header does not make it "more RESTful" regardless of how many people seem to think that is the case. It just makes it more "HTTPish" than defining your own pagination metadata.

11. Documentation

11.1 Introduction

Regardless of whether you decide to keep an API private or release it to the general public, documentation is incredibly important.

In the very early stages of development, some API developers will rely solely on a Postman collection (discussed in Chapter 8: Debugging) to be a sufficient source of documentation for their API. This may be the case, but as soon as the API is in use by more people than just the one developer with their one collection, this quickly becomes a nightmare.

Even if the API is in use internally, without a single source of regularly updated documentation for your API, you will be answering nonstop questions from anyone using it.

If the API is public then… well, without documentation nobody will use your API at all, which could drastically affect the successes of your company. Integration with services via an API is a very important factor for many companies these days, from startups to huge corporations, so do not go through the trouble of building something amazing only to have it completely ignored due to a lack of documentation.

11.2 Types of Documentation

There should be a few different types of documentation:

API Reference

The "API Reference" is sometimes referred to as "Endpoint Reference". This is essentially a list of all endpoints (and their associated HTTP Methods), descriptions of what they do and a list of all arguments that can be passed, with descriptions about what values work and in what format those values could be. That is a lot of work, but it can be made easier with some tools. More on that later.

Sample Code

"Sample Code" is generally just a case of building one or two libraries or code packages in different languages, documenting *their* API with tools like phpDocumentor[1], and showing lots of common scenarios covering the basics of how that code works. Examples could include "Search venues by name" and "Create a check-in with a photograph". These examples reduce the mental barrier for a developer because they can see concrete examples in a language familiar to them, instead of being forced to think in terms of HTTP requests.

Despite your own personal preferences, please, for the love of every god in the world, make your sample code look as good as you can in each language. Words cannot express how frustrating it is when some Ruby developer smashes out some *awful* PHP code – because they are bad with PHP – and passes that off as a finished product.

Regardless of the language, most sample code should look very similar. This has the benefit of letting users switch between languages without having to learn a new code package from scratch. PHP, Ruby and Python all have blocks or callbacks, objects and hashes, support variadics and have some concept of namespaces. One day, PHP will also support named parameters. One day.

Guides or Tutorials

This is the easiest of the lot. Take a subject like "Authentication" and talk through it like a blog post. Images, diagrams, code examples of the libraries handling various situations in one or multiple languages using tabs, etc. Some people show examples using command line curl, but that can get pretty nasty as curl is not exactly known for being an interface full of sugar.

A great example of a set of tutorials is the SoundCloud API[2]. Their "Using the API" page is a central resource which links to the API Reference, for those who want to get their hands dirty; it also contains simple scenarios like 'Uploading Audio Files' in multiple languages.

---

[1]http://phpdoc.org/
[2]http://developers.soundcloud.com/docs/api/guide

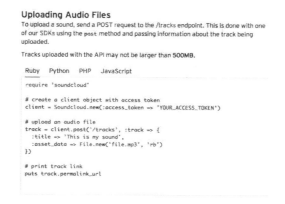

SoundCloud API Documentation – "Using the API"

If you check out the examples here, Ruby, Python and PHP all look nearly identical (although I am not sure what happened to JavaScript).

Writing these guides takes a bit of time, but that time will be given back in buckets, saving you answering the same questions over and over again. The other time saver is for when future you forgets how things work in three months, or you come back from a holiday rather frazzled and need a tutorial to guide you through how things work. The amount of times I have Google searched a problem and found a blog I have written a few months ago answering it… it happens.

There are plenty of great tools around for static text-based documentation like this. Generally any Markdown -> HTML static site generator works well; Sculpin[3] (PHP), Jekyll[4] (Ruby) and Hyde[5] (Python) all do this as well as each other.

11.3 Picking a Tool

There are no doubt multiple tools out there for generating your API/Endpoint documentation. Some recommend a system called Swagger[6], which is a great looking tool and works with a *huge* array of languages. Sadly, to me it seems to be somewhat of a black art.

[3]https://sculpin.io
[4]https://github.com/jekyll/jekyll
[5]http://ringce.com/hyde
[6]https://helloreverb.com/developers/swagger

Swagger defines a specification and various language or framework specific implementations come up with their own solution. For PHP, the way you go about this is through a rather confusing (and poorly documented) set of annotations with strange names. Furthermore, it requires you to distribute these annotations throughout a large chunk of your application, including data mapper style models, which you might not even have. It wanted property level annotations, and neither my models or Fractal transformers have properties, so this was a wild and wacky way to try and work.

Another tool called API Blueprint[7] takes care of this nicely. A company called Apiary[8] released this tool as open-source, and as their entire company is about API generation, it seems like rather a good fit.

11.4 Setting up API Blueprint and Aglio

API Blueprint has a very easy to understand set of Getting Started instructions[9], which has a series of approaches to creating your documentation with various languages and tool combinations. They are working on a Ruby utility and .NET seems to be covered. Sublime Text has a plugin[10], but by far the easiest is the command-line executable called Aglio[11].

There is one caveat — this tool uses NodeJS. That sounds like a blocker to some but it should not be. Only the command-line utility requires NodeJS, much like some command-line tools require Ruby or Python. Install NodeJS and move along to the next bit.

Step 1: Install NodeJS

If you are using OSX then Homebrew[12] makes this very easy:

```
1   $ brew install node
```

[7] http://apiary.io/blueprint
[8] http://apiary.io
[9] http://apiblueprint.org/#get-started
[10] https://github.com/apiaryio/api-blueprint-sublime-plugin
[11] https://github.com/danielgtaylor/aglio
[12] http://brew.sh

Otherwise the NodeJS[13] website has instructions for your operating system.

Step 2: Install Aglio

Install this utility as a command-line executable:

```
1   $ npm install -g aglio
```

The -g switch installs the utility globally, instead of just into the current folder.

Step 3: Generate Example Docs with Aglio

The sample code for the book includes the Aglio example Markdown file that will help to illustrate how easy it is to generate documentation HTML:

```
1   $ cd ~/apisyouwonthate/chapter11/aglio-example
2   $ aglio -i example.md -o index.html
```

Step 4: Generate HTML and Open in Browser

Create some sort of web server (XAMPP, WAMP, MAMP, Pow, shove it on FTP or whatever) and view the contents. This book has used PHP as an example before, so let us continue that trend:

```
1   $ php -S localhost:8001
```

Now browse to that address in your favourite browser and you should see some very attractive sample output.

---

[13]http://nodejs.org

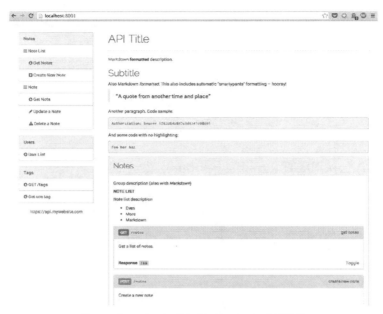

Example output of Aglio generated HTML

Looks amazing, right?

Step 5: Find a Plugin

Writing Markdown then switching over to the terminal and running a command can be a tricky workflow, so try and find a plugin for an editor you like which can help. If you use Atom[14] then there is an Atom plugin[15] you can use, but there are doubtless other options available.

11.5 Learning API Blueprint Syntax

To make the output reflect your API documentation, the Markdown source files will need updating. While they are generally just Markdown, there is a specific format to this, known as "API Blueprint format 1A".

Go to the following location and open up `example.md`:

---

[14] https://atom.io/
[15] https://atom.io/packages/api-blueprint-preview

```
1  $ cd ~/apisyouwonthate/chapter11/place-example
```

The rest of this section will walk through this `example.md` and explain what various parts mean.

Metadata

This is simple. The API title, URL, introduction, etc. is just some Markdown:

Very start of an API Blueprint markdown file, showing metadata

```
1  FORMAT: 1A
2  HOST: https://api.example.com
3
4  # FakeSquare API
5
6  This is documentation for the theoretical check-in app API that has been built
7  throughout the book [Build APIs You Won't Hate].
8
9  [Build APIs You Won't Hate]: https://leanpub.com/build-apis-you-wont-hate
10
11 ## Authorization
12
13 This could be anything, but it seems like a good place
14 to explain how access tokens work.
15
16 Most endpoints in the FakeSquare API will require the `Authorization` HTTP header.
17
18 ```http
19 Authorization: bearer vr5HmMkzlxKE70W1y4MibiJUusZwZC25NOVBEx3BD1
20 ```
21
22 Failing to do so will cause the following error:
23
24 ```json
25 {
26   "error" : {
27     "code" : "GEN-MAYBGTFO",
28     "http_code" : 401,
29     "message" : "Unauthorized"
30   }
```

```
31  }
32  ```
33
34  Or something. This is mostly just an introduction, so provide links to tutorial
35  sections elsewhere on your site.
```

A very quick and easy introduction showing the name of the API (FakeSquare API) and a basic example of how to authenticate a request with our API.

Resource Groups

To keep this simple but also cover a lot of different usages, we will take examples from the action plan in Chapter 2: Planning and Creating Endpoints for Places, and document them in API Blueprint syntax.

> Places
> - Create
> - Read
> - Update
> - Delete
> - List (lat, lon, distance or box)
> - Image

Using the same logic in chapter 2 as we used to outline the user endpoints, we can assume these endpoints:

Action	Endpoint
Create	POST /places
Read	GET /places/X
Update	PUT /places/X
Delete	DELETE /places/X
List	GET /places
Image	PUT /places/X/image

Everything at or below the /places level is considered a "Resource Group" by API Blueprint, so our new example will only have one group.

```
1   # Group Places
2   Search and manage places.
```

That first line has the reserved keyword `Group` that will be removed from output. The `Places` is the name of the group. The line below is an optional description for humans.

In a real API you would have more groups. `Users`, `Check-ins`, `Posts`, etc.

Resources

API Blueprint accepts multiple resource sections per group section, and considers /places, /places/X and /places/X/image to be different resources. You probably consider /places to be more of a collection of resources, and consider /places/X/image to be a subresource, but API Blueprint considers them all "Resources".

Not a problem. Simply make some h2 tags using the `##` prefix:

Example outline of multiple 'Resource Sections'.

```
1   ## Place List [/places{?lat}{&lon}{&distance}{&box}{&number}{&page}]
2
3
4   ## Create new place [/places]
5
6
7   ## Places [/places/{id}]
8   Manage an existing place.
9
10
11  ## Place Images [/places/{id}/image]
12  Places can have an image associated with them, which will act as a cover photo
13  or photograph.
```

Here we have four "Resource Sections", each for a different resource. The one oddity here is that there are two entries for /places. The reasoning here is that each "Resource Group" has its own "URI Template". No two groups can have the same template (two with /places would error) and if you want to document parameters then you need to put them in the template.

It seems odd, but just go with it.

1. One resource section for listing (with the filter/query/search parameters listed)
2. One resource section for creating a new item on a collection
3. One resource section for a single item
4. One resource section for each and every subresource your API may
   have on an item

Resource Actions

Actions are what you would expect them to be – the actions outlined in
the action plan.

You can spot an action in two ways. Firstly due to the h3 header (###) and
secondly by the trailing [GET] HTTP verb notation.

Example of the 'Place List' resource using API Blueprint Markdown

```
1   ## Place List [/places{?lat}{&lon}{&distance}{&box}{&number}{&page}]
2
3   ### Get places [GET]
4   Locate places close to a certain set of coordinates, or provide a box of coordinates \
5   to search within.
6
7   + Parameters
8
9       + lat (optional, number, `40.7641`) ... Latitude to search near, with any accuracy
10      + lon (optional, number, `-73.9866`) ... Longitude to search near, with any accur\
11  acy
12      + distance = `10` (optional, number, `20`) ... The radius size in miles to search\
13    for from lat and lon coordinates
14      + box (optional, string, `40.7641,-73.9866,40.7243,-73.9841`) ... Top left latitu\
15  de, top left longitude, bottom right latitude, bottom right longitude
16      + number (optional, integer, `15`) ... The number of results to return per page
17      + page = `1` (optional, integer, `15`) ... Which page of the result data to return
18
19  + Response 200 (application/json)
20
21          {
22              "data": [
```

```
23                    {
24                        "id": 2,
25                        "name": "Videology",
26                        "lat": 40.713857,
27                        "lon": -73.961936,
28    *                   "created_at": "2013-04-02"
29                    },
30                    {
31                        "id": 1,
32                        "name": "Barcade",
33                        "lat": 40.712017,
34                        "lon": -73.950995,
35                        "created_at": "2012-09-23"
36                    }
37                ]
38            }
```

This is the first resource section, now filled out. It lists the available parameters for the URL with a very special syntax:

```
1   + <parameter name>: `<example value>` (<type> | enum[<type>], required | optional)
2     - <description>
3
4       <additional description>
5
6       + Default: `<default value>`
7
8       + Members
9           + `<enumeration value 1>` - <enumeration description 1>
10          + `<enumeration value 2>` - <enumeration description 2>
11          ...
12          + `<enumeration value N>` - <enumeration description N>
```

Our example has used slightly shorter syntax and skipped the additional description and enum values, but it takes advantage of much of the first line.

```
1   + lat: `40.7641` (number, optional) - Latitude to search near, with any accuracy
```

This explains that the field is numeric, it is optional, and shows an example value of 40.7641.

```
1  + page: `1` (integer, optional) - Which page of the result data to return
2      + Default: `15`
```

Similar, but this time a default value has been added which in the case of pagination will probably be 1.

The rest of this action section is responses.

Show an example response for a specific content type.

```
1  + Response 200 (application/json)
2
3          { ... }
```

This says that you can expect a 200 status, which will be Content-Type: application/json and shows an example of the body content.

Now if we run Aglio again and serve it up through a web server:

```
1  $ aglio -i example.md -o index.html
2  $ php -S localhost:8001
```

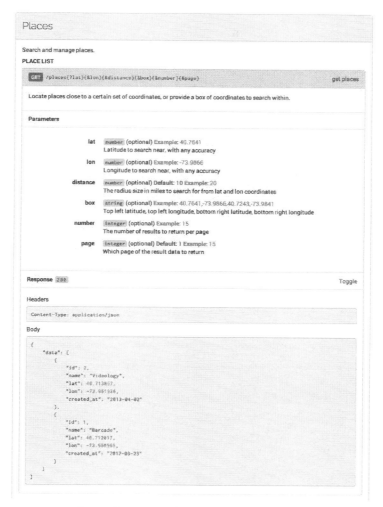

Example output of Aglio generated HTML

How amazing is that for such a little amount of Markdown? Doing all of that manually would certainly not be any fun.

Requests

Documenting the request content and offering examples is, of course, one of the most important parts of any API documentation and API Blueprint does not disappoint.

API Blueprint will allow you to create multiple request examples for an action. Looking at the `Place Images` resource will outline how this is done:

Example of the 'Place Images' resource.

```
1   ## Place Images [/places/{id}/image]
2   Places can have an image associated with them, which will act as a cover photo
3   or photograph.
4
5   + Parameters
6
7       + id (integer, required) - The unique identifier of a place
8
9   ### Set place image [PUT]
10  Assign a new image or replace the existing image for a place.
11
12  + Request (image/gif)
13
14      + Headers
15              Authorization: Bearer {access token}
16      + Body
17              <raw source of gif file>
18
19  + Request (image/jpeg)
20
21      + Headers
22              Authorization: Bearer {access token}
23      + Body
24              <raw source of jpeg file>
25
26  + Request (image/png)
27
28      + Headers
29
30              Authorization: Bearer {access token}
31      + Body
32
33              <raw source of png file>
```

Here the `<raw source of png file>` stuff is just plain-text – because pasting in the contents of an actual PNG file would not look great – but you can use JSON or anything else.

Having multiple request examples can be very important if you are unfortunate enough to be documenting an API which supports more than one input format, like JSON and XML for instance.

Responses

Each endpoint in your API will have one or more different responses. There will probably be one or more 20xs, some 40xs, and maybe a few 50xs too.

An action response section with multiple error responses.

```
1   + Response 400 (application/json)
2
3           {
4             "error" : {
5               "code": "GEN-FUBARGS",
6               "http_code" : 400,
7               "message": "Content-Type must be image/png, image/jpg or image/gif"
8             }
9           }
10
11  + Response 404 (application/json)
12
13          {
14            "error" : {
15              "code" : "GEN-LIKETHEWIND",
16              "http_code" : 404,
17              "message" : "Resource Not Found"
18            }
19          }
```

A tricky thing here is that while your API might return a `400` code for multiple reasons, API Blueprint will not be happy about having multiple responses listed with the same HTTP code.

This is only thrown in as a warning, and may only be related to Aglio and not API Blueprint itself, as the documentation seems to display fine. Either put multiple body examples next to each other or add multiple response items with the same code and ignore the warnings.

11.6 Further Reading

The `example.md` file provided contains more examples than highlighted in this chapter.

There is more to learn on the API Blueprint repository[16], including more examples[17]. Their wiki has extensive documentation of the API Blueprint Format syntax[18] too.

Between this chapter and those articles, you should be documenting your own APIs within no time.

---

[16] https://github.com/apiaryio/api-blueprint
[17] https://github.com/apiaryio/api-blueprint/tree/master/examples
[18] https://github.com/apiaryio/api-blueprint/wiki/API-Blueprint-Roadmap

12. HATEOAS

12.1 Introduction

HATEOAS is a tricky subject to explain, but it is actually rather simple. It stands for Hypermedia as the Engine of Application State, and is pronounced as either *hat-ee-os*, *hate O-A-S* or *hate-ee-ohs*; the latter of which sounds a little like a cereal for API developers.

However you want to try and say it, it basically means two things for your API:

1. Content negotiation
2. Hypermedia controls

In my experience, content negotiation is one of the first things many API developers implement. When building my CodeIgniter Rest-Server extension, it was the first feature I added, because hey, it is fun! Changing the `Accept` header and seeing the `Content-Type` header in the response switch from JSON to XML or CSV is great, and also super easy to do.

12.2 Content Negotiation

Some self-proclaimed RESTful APIs (Twitter, you are to blame for this) handle content negotiation with file extensions. Their URLs often look like:

- `/statuses/show.json?id=210462857140252672`
- `/statuses/show.xml?id=210462857140252672`

This is a bit of a misuse of the concept of a resource and forces users to know not only that the endpoint show exists, but that they must pick a content type extension and that the `id` parameter must be used.

A good API would simply have /statuses/210462857140252672. This has the dual benefit of letting the API respond with a default content type, or respecting the Accept header and either outputting the request content type or spitting out a 415 status code if the API does not support it. The second benefit is that the consumer does not need to know about ?id=.

URIs are not supposed to be a bunch of folders and file names and an API is not a list of JSON files or XML files. They are a list of resources that can be represented in different formats depending on the Accept header, **and nothing else**.

A simple example of content negotiation requesting JSON

```
1   GET /places HTTP/1.1
2   Host: localhost:8000
3   Accept: application/json
```

A response would then contain JSON if the API supports JSON as an output format.

A shortened example of the HTTP response with JSON data

```
1    HTTP/1.1 200 OK
2    Host: localhost:8000
3    Connection: close
4
5    {
6        "data": [
7            {
8                "id": 1,
9                "name": "Mireille Rodriguez",
10               "lat": -84.147236,
11               "lon": 49.254065,
12               "address1": "12106 Omari Wells Apt. 801",
13               "address2": "",
14               "city": "East Romanberg",
15               "state": "VT",
16               "zip": 20129,
17               "website": "http://www.torpdibbert.com/",
18               "phone": "(029)331-0729x4259"
19           },
20           ...
```

```
21       ]
22   }
```

Most popular APIs will support JSON by default, or maybe *only* JSON as our sample app has done so far. This is not realistic, but has been done throughout the book so far, mainly for the sake of simplicity.

XML is still a tricky one to do as you need to require view files, and that is out of scope of this chapter.

YAML, however, is rather easy to achieve, so we can see how content negotiation works with a little change to our app.

Check ~/apisyouwonthate/chapter12/ for the updated sample app.

The main change other than including the Symfony YAML component[1] was to simply update the respondWithArray() method to check the Accept header and react accordingly.

Updated respondWithArray() method with accept header detection

```
1   protected function respondWithArray(array $array, array $headers = [])
2   {
3       // You will probably want to do something intelligent with charset if provided.
4       // This chapter just ignores everything and takes the main MIME type value
5
6       $mimeParts = (array) explode(';', Input::server('HTTP_ACCEPT'));
7       $mimeType = strtolower($mimeParts[0]);
8
9       switch ($mimeType) {
10          case 'application/json':
11              $contentType = 'application/json';
12              $content = json_encode($array);
13              break;
14
15          case 'application/x-yaml':
16              $contentType = 'application/x-yaml';
17              $dumper = new YamlDumper();
18              $content = $dumper->dump($array, 2);
19              break;
20
```

[1]http://symfony.com/doc/current/components/yaml/introduction.html

```
21         default:
22             $contentType = 'application/json';
23             $content = json_encode([
24                 'error' => [
25                     'code' => static::CODE_INVALID_MIME_TYPE,
26                     'http_code' => 406,
27                     'message' => sprintf('Content of type %s is not supported.', $mim\
28 eType),
29                 ]
30             ]);
31     }
32
33     $response = Response::make($content, $this->statusCode, $headers);
34     $response->header('Content-Type', $contentType);
35
36     return $response;
37 }
```

Very basic, but now if we try a different MIME type we can expect a
different result:

An HTTP request specifying the preferred response MIME type

```
1 GET /places HTTP/1.1
2 Host: localhost:8000
3 Accept: application/x-yaml
```

The response will be in YAML.

A shortened example of the HTTP response with YAML data

```
1 HTTP/1.1 200 OK
2 Host: localhost:8000
3 Connection: close
4
5 data:
6     - { id: 1, name: 'Mireille Rodriguez', lat: -84.147236, lon: 49.254065, address1:\
7  '12106 Omari Wells Apt. 801', address2: '', city: 'East Romanberg', state: VT, zip: \
8 20129, website: 'http://www.torpdibbert.com/', phone: (029)331-0729x4259 }
9     ...
```

Making these requests programmatically is simple.

Using PHP and the Guzzle package to request a different response type

```php
1  use GuzzleHttp\Client;
2
3  $client = new Client(['base_url' => 'http://localhost:8000']);
4
5  $response = $client->get('/places', [
6      'headers' => ['Accept' => 'application/x-yaml']
7  ]);
8
9  $response->getBody(); // YAML, ready to be parsed
```

This is not the end of the conversation for content negotiation as there is more to talk about with vendor-based MIME types for resources, which can also be versioned. To keep this chapter on point, that discussion will happen in Chapter 13: API Versioning.

12.3 Hypermedia Controls

The second part of HATEOAS, however, is drastically underused, and is the last step in making your API technically a RESTful API.

Batman provides a standard response to often futile bucket remark "But it's not RESTful if you..." Credit to Troy Hunt (@troyhunt)

While you often hear complaints like "but that is not RESTful!" from people about silly things, this is one instance where they are completely right. Roy Fielding says that without hypermedia controls an API is not RESTful[2], writing back in 2008. People have been ignoring that ever since, and the last estimate was that 74% of APIs claiming to be "RESTful" do not actually use hypermedia.

---

[2]http://roy.gbiv.com/untangled/2008/rest-apis-must-be-hypertext-driven

RESTful Nirvana

There is something floating around the REST/Hypermedia community called the Richardson Maturity Model[3], written about here by Martin Fowler[4] but originally invented by Leonard Richardson[5]. It covers what he considers to be 'the four levels of REST':

1. **"The Swamp of POX."** You're using HTTP to make RPC calls. HTTP is only really used as a tunnel.
2. **Resources.** Rather than making every call to a service endpoint, you have multiple endpoints that are used to represent resources, and you're talking to them. This is the very beginnings of supporting REST.
3. **HTTP Verbs.** This is the level that something like Rails gives you out of the box: You interact with these Resources using HTTP verbs, rather than always using POST.
4. **Hypermedia Controls.** HATEOAS. You're 100% REST compliant.
   – **Source:** Steve Klabnik, "Haters gonna HATEOAS"[6]

Some dispute this model because, as Roy says, unless you have hypermedia then it is not REST. The model is good as long as you understand that steps 1, 2 and 3 are still "not REST" and step 4 is "REST".

So, what are hypermedia controls? They are just links to other content, relationships, and further actions. These allow a consumer to browse around the API, discovering actions as it goes.

Basically, your data needs to have "hyperlinks", which you have probably been using in your HTML output for years. I said early on in the book that REST is just using the same conventions as the actual Internet, instead of inventing new ones, so it makes sense that linking to other resources should be the same in an API as it is in a web page.

The general underlying theme of hypermedia is that an API should be able to make perfect sense to an API client application and the human looking

---

[3]http://martinfowler.com/articles/richardsonMaturityModel.html
[4]http://martinfowler.com/
[5]http://www.crummy.com/
[6]http://timelessrepo.com/haters-gonna-hateoas

at the responses, entirely without having to hunt through documentation to work out what is going on.

Small HATEOAS concepts have been sneakily sprinkled throughout this book, from suggesting error codes be combined with human readable error messages and documentation links, to helping the client application avoid maths when interacting with pagination. The underlying theme is always to make controls such as next, previous (or any other sort of related interaction) clearly obvious to either a human or a computer.

Understanding Hypermedia Controls

This is the easiest part of building a RESTful API, so I am going to try really hard not to leave this section at "just add links mate" (my normal advice for anyone asking about HATEOAS).

Our usual data is output in such a way that only represents one or more resources. By itself, this one piece of data is an island, completely cut off from the rest of the API. The only way to continue interacting with the API is for the developer to read the documentation and understand what data can be related, and to discover where that data might live. This is far from ideal.

To tie one `place` to the related resources, subresources or collections is easy.

```
1   {
2       "data": [
3           "id": 1,
4           "name": "Mireille Rodriguez",
5           "lat": -84.147236,
6           "lon": 49.254065,
7           "address1": "12106 Omari Wells Apt. 801",
8           "address2": "",
9           "city": "East Romanberg",
10          "state": "VT",
11          "zip": 20129,
12          "website": "http://www.torpdibbert.com/",
13          "phone": "(029)331-0729x4259",
14          "links": [
15                  {
```

```
16                              "rel": "self",
17                              "uri": "/places/2"
18                  },
19                  {
20                              "rel": "place.checkins",
21                              "uri": "/places/2/checkins"
22                  },
23                  {
24                              "rel": "place.image",
25                              "uri": "/places/2/image"
26                  }
27          ]
28      ]
29 }
```

Here are three simple entries, with the first linking to itself. They all contain a `uri` (Universal Resource Indicator) and a `rel` (Relationship).

URI vs. URL

The acronym "URI" is often used to refer to only content after the protocol, hostname and port (meaning URI is the path, extension and query string), whilst "URL" is used to describe the full address. While this is not strictly true, it is perpetuated by many software projects such as CodeIgniter. Wikipedia[7] and the W3[8] say a bunch of conflicting things, but I feel like a URI is easily described as being simply any sort of identifier for the location of a resource on the Internet.

A URI can be partial, or absolute. URL is considered by some to be a completely non-existent term, but this book uses URL to describe an absolute URI, which is what you see in the address bar. Rightly or wrongly. Got it?

Some people scoff at the `self` relationship suggesting that it is pointless. While you certainly know what URL you just called, that URL is not always going to match up with the `self` URI. For example, if you just created a `place` resource, you will have called POST `/places`, and that is not what you would want to call again to get updated information on the same

---

[7]http://wikipedia.org/wiki/Uniform_Resource_Identifier
[8]http://www.w3.org/TR/uri-clarification/

resource. Regardless of the context, outputting a place always needs to have a self relationship, and that self should not just output whatever is in the address bar. Basically put, the self relationship points to where the resource lives, not the current address.

As for the other rel items, they are links to subresources that contain related information. The content of the tags can be anything you like, just keep it consistent throughout. The convention used in this example is to namespace relationships so that they are unique. Two different types of resources could have a checkins relationship (eg: users and places), so keeping them unique could be of benefit for the sake of documentation at least. Maybe you would prefer to remove the namespace, but that is up to you.

Those custom relationships have fairly unique names, but for more generic relationships you can consider using the Registry of Link Relations[9] defined by the IANA, which is used by Atom (RFC 4287[10]) and plenty of other things.

Creating Hypermedia Controls

This is literally a case of shoving some links into your data output. However you chose to do that, it can be part of your "transformation" or "presentation" layer.

If you are using the PHP component Fractal – which has been used as an example throughout the book – then you can simply do the following:

PlaceTransformer with links included in the response data.

```
public function transform(Place $place)
{
    return [
        'id'        => (int) $place->id,
        'name'      => $place->name,
        'lat'       => (float) $place->lat,
        'lon'       => (float) $place->lon,
        'address1'  => $place->address1,
        'address2'  => $place->address2,
```

[9] http://www.iana.org/assignments/link-relations/link-relations.xhtml
[10] http://atompub.org/rfc4287.html

```
10          'city'            => $place->city,
11          'state'           => $place->state,
12          'zip'             => $place->zip,
13          'website'         => $place->website,
14          'phone'           => $place->phone,
15
16          'links'           => [
17              [
18                  'rel' => 'self',
19                  'uri' => '/places/'.$place->id,
20              ],
21              [
22                  'rel' => 'place.checkins',
23                  'uri' => '/places/'.$place->id.'/checkins',
24              ],
25              [
26                  'rel' => 'place.image',
27                  'uri' => '/places/'.$place->id.'/image',
28              ]
29          ],
30      ];
31  }
```

People try to get smarter and have various relationships based on their $_SERVER settings or based on their ORM relationships, but all of that is just going to cause you problems. If you have these transformers then you only need to write this lot out once. This then avoids exposing any database logic and keeps your code readable and understandable.

Once you have input these links, other people need to know how to interact with them. You might think, "surely I should put GET or PUT in there so people know what to do". Wrong. They are links to resources, not actions. An image exists for a place, and we can either blindly assume we can make certain actions on it, or we can ask our API what actions are available and cache the result.

Discovering Resources Programmatically

Taking a shortened example from earlier on in this chapter, we can expect to see output like this:

```
1   {
2       "data": [
3               ...
4           "links": [
5                   {
6                           "rel": "self",
7                           "uri": "/places/2"
8                   },
9                   {
10                          "rel": "place.checkins",
11                          "uri": "/places/2/checkins"
12                  },
13                  {
14                          "rel": "place.image",
15                          "uri": "/places/2/image"
16                  }
17          ]
18      ]
19  }
```

We can assume that a GET will work on both the self and the place.checkins endpoints, but what else can we do with them? Beyond that, what on Earth do we do with the place.image endpoint?

HTTP has us covered here with a simple and effective verb that has so far not been discussed: OPTIONS.

An HTTP request using the OPTIONS verb

```
1   OPTIONS /places/2/checkins HTTP/1.1
2   Host: localhost:8000
```

The response to the previous HTTP request

```
1   HTTP/1.1 200 OK
2   Host: localhost:8000
3   Connection: close
4   Allow: GET,HEAD,POST
```

By inspecting the Allow header, we as humans (or programmatically as an API client application), can work out what options are available to us on any given endpoint. This is what JavaScript is often doing in your browser for AJAX requests and you might not even know it.

Doing this programmatically is pretty easy too, and most HTTP clients in any given language will let you make an OPTIONS call just as easily as making a GET or POST call. If your HTTP client does not let you do this, then change your HTTP client.

Making an OPTIONS HTTP request using PHP and the Guzzle package

```
1  use GuzzleHttp\Client;
2
3  $client = new Client(['base_url' => 'http://localhost:8000']);
4  $response = $client->options('/places/2/checkins');
5  $methods = array_walk('trim', explode(',', $response->getHeader('Accept')));
6  var_dump($methods); // Outputs: ['GET', 'HEAD', 'POST']
```

So in this instance, we know that we can get a list of check-ins for a place using GET and we can add to them by making a POST HTTP request to that URL. We can also do a HEAD check, which is the same as a GET but skips the HTTP body. You will probably need to handle this differently in your application, but this is handy for checking if a resource or collection exists without having to download the entire body content (i.e: just look for a 200 or a 404).

It might seem a little nuts to take this extra step to interact with an API, but really it should be considered much easier than hunting for documentation. Think about it: trying to find that little "Developers" link on the website, then navigating to the documentation for the correct API (because they are so cool they have about three), then wondering if you have the right version... not fun. Compare that to a programmatically self-documenting API, which can grow, change and expand over time, rename URLs and... well that is a real win. Trust me.

If you know that an API follows RESTful principles then you *should* be confident that it follows HATEOAS because advertising it as RESTful without following HATEOAS is a big stinking lie. Sadly, most of the popular APIs out there are big stinking liars.

> GitHub responds with a 500, Reddit with 501 Not Implemented, Google maps with 405 Method Not Allowed. You get the idea.

I've tried many others, and the results are usually similar. Sometimes it yields something identical to a GET response. None of these are right.
– **Source:** Zac Stewart, "The HTTP OPTIONS method and potential for self-describing RESTful APIs"[11]

If you are building your own API, then you can easily do this yourself and your clients know that you know how to build a decent API.

And that, is about all there is for HATEOAS. You should now know enough to go out and build up an API that in theory you won't hate. Sadly, you will probably need to build a new version within a few months regardless, so for that we will now take a look at API versioning.

[11]http://zacstewart.com/2012/04/14/http-options-method.html

13. API Versioning

13.1 Introduction

Once you have built your wonderful new API, at some point it will need to be replaced or have new features added. Sadly, there is no real consensus on what approach is the best, but instead there are pros and cons to each approach.

The general advice you will find most experts giving is this: try to limit change as much as possible. That is a very fair statement to make, but also seems like a bit of a cop out. Regardless of how well planned your API is, your business requirements will likely be what forces you to make substantial changes eventually.

This can be a killer in the startup world, where things are considerably less structured. Kapture started off with "opportunities" which became "photo opps" and ended up being called "campaigns". You can laugh at that and say it will never happen to you, but it will. When you are least expecting it, business requirements will come at you like a wet mackerel to the face. When that happens, API versioning is often the only solution.

> Sure, you could say that your API needs to maintain backward compatibility, but that is not very realistic when you are reusing your API properly across your product line. To demonstrate further, let us say you have 30 applications (and maybe a handful of external companies using the API), all of which are relying on the "customer" REST resource. Your choices now are:
>
> 1. Keep it backward compatible (and lose the million dollar sale because you could not implement cool feature X)
> 2. Change all 30 applications simultaneously to handle the new data (you likely do not have enough resource to do this and deliver on time)

3. Make the change, breaking the apps you do not have time
   to upgrade, but get the sale. (Of course, you will fix the
   remaining apps in the future, right?)
   – **Source:** Jeremy Highley, "Versioning and Types in REST/HTTP
   API Resources"[1]

13.2 Different Approaches to API Versioning

As has been done in several other chapters, this chapter will outline several different approaches and list their pros and cons. In other chapters,
the final suggestion is generally implied to be a "better" solution, but in
this chapter they are all compromises. Some are technically RESTful but
incredibly complicated to implement; they are also complicated for your
users. This means you have to put some real thought into the approach.

Throughout this chapter will be references to various popular services
with public APIs and the type of API versioning they use. Credit goes
to Tim Wood for compiling an extensive list in "How are REST APIs
versioned?"[2], which will be used for reference in this chapter.

Approach #1: URI

Throwing a version number in the URI is a very common practice amongst
popular public APIs.

Essentially, all you do here is put a 'v1' or '1' in the URL, so that the next
version can be easily changed.

    https://api.example.com/v1/places

Due to being so prolific throughout various public APIs, this is often the
first approach API developers take when building their own. It is by far
the easiest and it does the job.

Twitter has two versions, '/1/' and '/1.1/', both of which were live at the
time of writing. This gives developers a chance to update any code that is

---

[1]http://thereisnorightway.blogspot.com.tr/2011/02/versioning-and-types-in-resthttp-api.html
[2]http://www.lexicalscope.com/blog/2012/03/12/how-are-rest-apis-versioned/

referencing the old endpoints, so they can use the new ones. Most APIs would have called it '/2/', but since it was not a drastic change, perhaps they wanted a more subtle number.

Some say that URI versioning allows for a more copy-and-paste-friendly URL than other approaches (many of which involve HTTP headers) and this is supposedly better for support.

That might be true in some ways but is not totally accurate. No REST/Hypermedia API is ever going to be entirely copy-and-paste-friendly because there will always be headers involved: `Cache-Control`, `Accept`, `Content-Type`, `Authorization`, etc. Trying to make an entire API request fit in a URL just seems like a fool's errand.

While the copy-paste argument is simply a lack of a positive, this versioning approach does have some potentially frustrating downsides.

The first thing people will say is that it is not technically RESTful. If you care about breaking this REST rule or not is up to you, but Roy Fielding says that placing the version in the URL like this basically makes your API into a RPC API instead.

 Roy T. Fielding
@fielding Following

The reason to make a real REST API is to get evolvability ... a "v1" is a middle finger to your API customers, indicating RPC/HTTP (not REST)

Roy says: "v1 is a middle finger to your API customers, indicating RPC/HTTP (not REST)"

His mention of "evolvability" is fundamental to the concept of REST. A resource is meant to be more like a permalink. This permalink (the URL) should never change. Over time you can hit that permalink with different version headers, or request different representations of JSON, or XML, or whatever you like, but it will always be the same URL.

If the Internet is built around linking together and those links are changing all the time then, well, things break. This might not be something you are too concerned about – especially if the API is internal – but it can be hugely annoying for others.

For example, if you store the URL of an endpoint in your database for later reference, it might look like this:

> https://api.example.com/v1/places/213

One day, you get an email from example.com stating that their v1 API is going to be deprecated in three months, and you need to start using the v2 API as soon as you can.

If you update your code to match the updated format with whatever new or renamed fields the new version may contain, then great, your new code will be ready to work with the new API version and you can start saving the new URL when you enter the record in your database. That works for new records, but you cannot leave the old records in there referencing the old API v1 URL.

So what do you do? One solution would be to string replace the old URL and hope the new URL is right:

> https://api.example.com/**v2**/places/213

That might have worked, if it was not for the fact that you missed the note in the email that says they no longer use auto-increment IDs in their URLs (they read that it was a bad idea somewhere) and have decided to use slugs instead:

> https://api.example.com/**v2**/places/taksim-bunk-hostel

Now what? The only solution here is to create a script that goes through each and every record in your database, hits their v1 API and gets information (hopefully that slug is available) and then constructs a 'v2' compatible URL to store.

If you do that with a few million records then you will probably hit some API limits fairly quickly. Twitter, for example, limits applications to 15 requests per endpoint per 15 minutes in some situations, so this would take about two weeks to update one million records.

Maybe that sounds like an edge case, but putting the API version in the URL is asking for all sorts of obscure problems down the line, and asking your developers to manually construct resource URLs with string replacement is just rude. Peter Williams pointed this out in an article titled "Versioning REST Web Services"[3] back in 2008, but everyone has been consistently ignoring him it seems.

Another downside to this approach is that pointing v1 and v2 to different servers can be difficult, unless you use some sort of Apache Proxy feature or nginx-as-a-proxy trickery. Generally speaking, most systems expect the same path to be on the same server (doing otherwise can lead to overhead), so if v1 is PHP and v2 is Scala, you can run into some trouble having them all set up on the same server.

The opposite of the putting-them-on-the-same-server-can-be-hard problem, is when API developers try to let one single code base take care of this versioning internally in their web app. They simply make routes with the prefix /v1/places, then when they want to make v2 they copy the routes, copy the controllers and tweak things. This *can* be done if you also version your transformers (to maintain structure and data types), and you are confident that all shared code (libraries, packages, etc.) will maintain a consistent output throughout. This is rarely the case, and people putting v1 in their URLs are just doing it because it is the only solution they know.

Instead, consider making each version its own code base. This means the code is totally separate, executed separately, with different web server vhosts or maybe even on different servers.

If the APIs are very similar (same language, same framework, etc), then you can simply share a Git history — be it different branch in the same api repository, or a different branch. Some people take the Git Flow[4] model and prepends version numbers, so one repository may have the following branches:

[3]http://barelyenough.org/blog/2008/05/versioning-rest-web-services/
[4]http://nvie.com/posts/a-successful-git-branching-model/

- 1.0/master
- 1.0/develop
- 2.0/master
- 2.0/develop

As long as you share a Git history, you can pull from the other repository or branch and merge changes from older versions to newer versions. This lets you fix bugs in multiple versions easily instead of copying and pasting between all of your controllers in the the same code base.

Popular APIs

- Bitly
- Disqus
- Dropbox
- Bing (lol)
- Etsy
- Foursquare
- Tumblr
- Twitter
- Yammer
- YouTube

Pros

- Incredibly simple for API developers
- Incredibly simple for API consumers
- Copy-and-pasteable URLs

Cons

- Not technically RESTful
- Tricky to separate onto different servers
- Forces API consumers to do weird stuff to keep links up-to-date

Approach #2: Hostname

Some API developers try to avoid the issues with server setup found with putting the version in the URI and simply put the version number in the hostname (or subdomain) instead:

https://api-v1.example.com/places

This does not really solve any of the other problems. Having it in the URL in general (URI or subdomain) shares all the same problems for API consumers, but it does at least reduce the chances of API developers trying to let one code base handle it all.

Pros

- Incredibly simple for API developers
- Incredibly simple for API consumers
- "Copy-and-paste-able" URLs
- Easy to use DNS to split versions over multiple servers

Cons

- Not technically RESTful
- Forces API consumers to do weird stuff to keep links up-to-date

Approach #3: Body and Query Params

If you are going to take the URI version out of the URL, then one of the two other places to put it is the HTTP body itself:

```
1  POST /places HTTP/1.1
2  Host: api.example.com
3  Content-Type: application/json
4
5  {
6      "version" : "1.0"
7  }
```

This solves the problem of URLs changing over time, but can lead to inconsistent experiences. If the API developer is posting JSON, or a similar data structure, then it is easy, but if they are posting with a Content-Type of image/png or even text/csv then this becomes very complicated very quickly.

Some suggest the solution to that problem is to move the parameter to the query string, but now the API version is in the URL again! Immediately, many of the problems of the first two approaches are back.

```
1  POST /places?version=1.0 HTTP/1.1
2  Host: api.example.com
3
4  header1,header2
5  value1,value2
```

This... just do something else. Many PHP frameworks ignore the query string under anything other than a GET request, which goes against the HTTP specification but is still common. Having this parameter that moves around inside different content types in the body or sometimes in the URL or even always in the URL, regardless of the HTTP Verb being used, is just confusing.

Popular APIs

- Netflix
- Google Data
- PayPal
- Amazon SQS

Pros

- Simple for API developers
- Simple for API consumers
- Keeps URLs the same when param is in the body
- Technically a bit more RESTful than putting version in the URI

Cons

- Different content types require different params, and some (like CSV) just do not fit
- Forces API consumers to do weird stuff to keep links up-to-date when the param is in the query string

Approach #4: Custom Request Header

So if the URL and the HTTP body is a bad place to put API version information, where else is left? Well, headers of course!

```
1  GET /places HTTP/1.1
2  Host: api.example.com
3  BadApiVersion: 1.0
```

This example was lifted from Mark Nottingham[5], who is the chair of the IEFT HTTPbis Working Group[6] at the time of writing. That group is in charge of revising HTTP 1.1 and working on HTTP 2.0. He has this to say about custom version headers:

> This is broken and wrong for a whole mess of reasons. Why?
>
> First, because the server's response depends on the version in the request header, it means that the response really needs to be:

---

[5]http://www.mnot.net/
[6]http://trac.tools.ietf.org/wg/httpbis/trac/wiki

```
1   HTTP/1.1 200 OK
2   BadAPIVersion: 1.1
3   Vary: BadAPIVersion
```

> Otherwise, intervening caches can give clients the wrong re-
> sponse (e.g. a 1.2 response to a 1.1 client, or vice versa).
> – **Source:** Mark Nottingham, "Bad HTTP API Smells: Version
> Headers"[7]

Without specifying the `Vary` header, it is hard for a cache system like
Varnish to know that somebody is asking for 1.0 because the URL is not
any different than somebody asking for 1.1 or 2.0. That can be a big
problem as API consumers asking for a specific version need to get that
version, not a different one.

Beyond that rather tricky caching issue, it is generally just annoying.
If you use a custom header, then API consumers need to go and look
at your documentation to remember which it is. Maybe it is `API-Version`
or `Foursquare-Version` or `X-Api-Version` or `Dave`. Who knows, and who can
remember?

Popular APIs

- Azure

Pros

- Simple for API consumers (if they know about headers)
- Keeps URLs the same
- Technically a bit more RESTful than putting version in the URI

Cons

- Cache systems can get confused
- API developers can get confused (if they do not know about headers)

---

[7]http://www.mnot.net/blog/2012/07/11/header_versioning

Approach #5: Content Negotiation

The Accept header is designed to ask the server to respond with a specific resource in a different format. Traditionally, many developers think of this in terms of only (X)HTML, JSON, Images, etc., but it can be more generic than that. If we can RESTfully ask for our data to come back with different content types having different syntax, then why not reuse exactly the same header for versions too.

GitHub follows the advice of many of the people named in this chapter so far, and uses the Accept header to return different Media Types.

> All GitHub media types look like this:
>
> ```
> application/vnd.github[.version].param[+json]
> ```
>
> The most basic media types the API supports are:
>
> ```
> application/json
> application/vnd.github+json
> ```
>
> – **Source:** GitHub, "Media Types"[8]

Basically if you ask for either of the following two MIME types, the result will be returned as JSON:

- `application/json`
- `application/vnd.github+json`

Without specifying further, they will show you the current default response, which at the time of writing is v3 but could at any time change to v4. They warn that if you do not specify the version then your apps will break; fair enough.

To specify the version, you must use the following:

```
1   Accept: application/vnd.github.v3+json
```

---

[8]https://developer.github.com/v3/media/

If the default switches to v4 at some point in the future, your application will continue to use v3.

This solves the caching problem, solves the URL manipulation problems of the URL-based versioning approaches, and is considered rather REST-ful, but it can confuse some developers. You could train them to get used to it, or perhaps stick with URL-based versioning, but it is semantically more correct and generally works very well. This was done at Kapture for the internal API and it worked without problems.

The only downside is one that is found with all the approaches mentioned so far: if you version the entire API as a whole, it becomes very hard for API developers to upgrade their applications. It could be that only 10% of the API has changed between versions, but changing the version of the entire API can scare developers. Even with a changelog, it is hard for the developer to know if their entire application is going to break completely when they switch over. Even an extensive test suite is not going to catch every issue with a third party service like this, because most developers use hardcoded JSON responses in their unit tests to mock interactions.

If changing the version of the whole API is too much, the only other option is to version parts of the API.

Popular APIs

- GitHub

Pros

- Simple for API consumers (if they know about headers)
- Keeps URLs the same
- HATEOAS-friendly
- Cache-friendly
- Sturgeon-approved

Cons

- API developers can get confused (if they do not know about headers)
- Versioning the WHOLE thing can confuse users (but this is the same with all previous approaches)

Approach #6: Content Negotiation for Resources

Generally accepted to be the proper HATEOAS approach, content negotiation for specific resources using media types is one of the most complex
solutions, but is a very scalable way to approach things. It solves the all-
or-nothing approach of versioning the entire API, but still lets breaking
changes be made to the API in a manageable way.

Basically, if GitHub were to do this, they would take their current media-
type and add an extra item:

```
1   Accept: application/vnd.github.user.v4+json
```

Alternatively, the `Accept` header is capable of containing arbitrary parameters.

```
1   Accept: application/vnd.github.user+json; version=4.0
```

This was suggested by Avdi Grimm[9] and written about in an article by
Steve Klabnik[10] called "Nobody Understands REST or HTTP"[11]. That whole
article, written in 2011, is a great rant containing lots of useful advice.
Again, most API developers seem to have ignored the advice or have
simply not known about it.

Picking between those two specific formats will no doubt have pros and
cons. Apparently, Rails is not able to pick up the latter (or at least could
not in 2011), but that should not be considered much of a reason.

The other argument for using the latter media type is that arbitrary
parameter names can have the same confusion as arbitrary version header
names, but developers can all just agree to just call it "version". Right?

Whichever way you end up specifying the header, the advantage is not
just specifying "I want the v4 API" but instead saying "I would like the
v4 version of a place(s)". Services that provide an API can email their
API consumers saying "We are updating the way 'places' work. Here is

---

[9]http://about.avdi.org/

[10]http://blog.steveklabnik.com/

[11]http://blog.steveklabnik.com/posts/2011-07-03-nobody-understands-rest-or-http#i_want_
my_api_to_be_versioned

an example of the resource, here is what you need to change; specify the new version when you are ready".

Partial updates like this ease third party efforts to upgrade applications, and the chances of leaving developers stranded on an older version becomes far less likely.

Popular APIs

- GitHub

Pros

- HATEOAS-friendly
- Cache-friendly
- Keeps URLs the same
- Easier upgrades for API consumers
- Can be one code base or multiple

Cons

- API consumers need to pay attention to versions
- Splitting across multiple code bases is not impossible, but it is hard
- Putting it in the same code base leads to accidental breakage, if transformers are not versioned

Approach #7: Feature Flagging

This approach is something that so far I have only seen done by Facebook and its Graph API. Their approach is interesting, but not as common as some of these other approaches.

Facebook do not version their entire API with simple numbers like anybody else does. They do not version their resources, and they do not allow you to request different versions with headers, parameters or anything else.

They essentially make a custom version for each single client application. The way this works is there are various feature flags, which they call "migrations". They put out a migration every few months, write a blog, email API developers about it, and ask those developers to log into the developer area on the Facebook platform to manage their application.

Basically, they warn you that things are going to break in a few months. They list all the changes and give you the chance to see if this will affect your application. If your application does not use an endpoint that is being changed, or they are removing a field your application does not use, then you can click "Enable" for the migration. From that point on, any interaction your application has with the Facebook Graph API will use the new format.

If you wait, eventually they will flip that switch regardless. This is considered a fair warning, and means they do not have to support an old version for years. Facebook simply maintain one version with a few feature flags and those flags exist for a few months before that old code is removed. If your application still uses the old format then it is just tough.

To me, this system has the most benefits. One tricky part is that getting the timing right for the changeover is hard on API consumers. If your code is live looking at the old style, then you cannot push new code for the new style, because it will be broken until you flip the switch. That might only be seconds, but if you have multiple applications then you have to update and deploy all of them within minutes (or seconds) and then flip the switch.

Realistically speaking, that is very hard to do, so you will end up with code having a lot of if statements ready to look for fields that may or may not be there depending on the version. That leads to lots of extra code which you have to remember to remove afterwards by shoving comment blocks throughout your code:

```
1  # @TODO Kill this when Facebook September 13 Migration is confirmed working
```

This is not insanely hard, but it can be complicated sometimes.

Generally speaking, the Feature Flag solution is the easiest for API consumers if the changes happen to hit a part of the API they do not care about. They do not need to be scared of changing to an entirely new version of the API, they know their code will work, and things seem safer. If they *do* require changes then... well a few if statements never really hurt anyone.

13.3 Ask Your Users

None of these will have a drastic impact on your business, especially if your API is internal. If you are creating a platform as big as Facebook, then maybe you need a solution as complex as theirs, but that is probably not the case.

My advice with versioning (as with most aspects of your API) is to know your audience. Twitter gets away with flagrant disregard for almost every single concept or principle that ever makes something RESTful whilst still calling it a REST API, so you can probably break a few rules too.

> If I may leave others considering how to version their APIs with a final thought: nobody will use your API until you've built it. Stop procrastinating. None of these are "bad" in any tangible sense, they're just different.
>
> They are all easily consumable, they all return the same result and none of them are likely to have any real impact on the success of your project.
>
> – **Source:** Troy Hunt, "Your API versioning is wrong, which is why I decided to do it 3 different wrong ways"[12]

The real truth is that all of the approaches are annoying in some ways, or technically 'unRESTful' in some respects, or difficult, or a combination of it all. You have to pick what is realistic for your project in both the difficulty of the implementation and the skill/knowledge level of your target audience.

---

[12]http://www.troyhunt.com/2014/02/your-api-versioning-is-wrong-which-is.html

Conclusion

Thank you for reading the whole way through this book. This was a large and complex topic I tried to turn into an interesting read with a little humour.

It has been a really enjoyable experience, and I have been blown away with the positive feedback. I have also received plenty of constructive criticism, which was mostly begging me to hire an editor. The PHP Editor at SitePoint gave the book a 4/5 star rating, saying:

> The one downside is that Phil can't spell to save his life.

This is true. I've been writing blogs for years, and that has not helped me. This experience very much has. I hired a good friend of mine as an editor and she has done an amazing job.

Now that this book is in paperback form as well as eBook, I do plan to change it less. I do, however, have some ideas for a second edition which may be released in early 2016.

A dilemma I am currently having is that any further explanation of RESTful / Hypermedia API development is just going to be paraphrasing content in the various HTTP 1.1 Specification RFCs. Hypermedia APIs respect as many aspects of the HTTP spec as possible, so headers like `Accept-Language`, `Expires`, `Etag`, `Retry-After`, etc., could be catered for. A whole book could be written about the HTTP specification itself, so it seems somewhat outside the scope of this book, but it has been commonly requested.

No matter what happens next with this book, this has been a great project. Not only was it a much needed break from writing code nonstop 24/7, but it has ended up helping me out substantially with my US visa! It has also helped me out a few times, when I forgot how something worked and looked back in here.

If this book has helped you out, please pass it on. Hand the paperback to somebody, or give them a link to apisyouwonthate.com, and help me continue to update the project. Part of the joys of this project are the extra income of course, but I really enjoy helping to educate people.

I am always happy to hand out coupon codes for people who want to give away cheap copies of the eBook at their usergroups, conferences, etc, so find me on twitter for that: @philsturgeon.

Thanks again for reading!

Further Reading

Here are some resources you should look into reading.

API Web Resources

Interagent: HTTP API Design[13] – HTTP API design guide extracted from work on the Heroku Platform API. They have some good tips for making a HTTP API. I don't agree with all of it entirely, but a lot of it it. Either way it gives you a lot of things to think about.

Nordic APIs[14] – Online API advice, with articles about new technologies in the world of APIs, opinion pieces and the occasional article about why SOAP is great sometimes.

Non-API Books

While these books are not directly about API development, they are about related subjects. APIs must be secure. APIs need to be tested. APIs need virtual machines to run on locally, servers to live on in production, and that all needs to be provisioned using fancy devops tooling.

Building Secure PHP Apps[15] – Is your PHP app truly secure? Let's make sure you get home on time and sleep well at night.

The Grumpy Programmer's PHPUnit Cookbook[16] – Learning how to use PH-PUnit doesn't have to suck. Your code is untested and fixing bugs is tedious. You know you need something better, but time just doesn't seem to be on your side. Making things "right" is costly and you need to deliver working code NOW.

---

[13] https://github.com/interagent/http-api-design
[14] http://nordicapis.com/
[15] https://leanpub.com/buildingsecurephpapps
[16] https://leanpub.com/grumpy-phpunit

Scaling PHP Apps[17] – Steve Corona's book about scaling not just PHP, but Nginx and various data stores helped me out a lot over the course of the Kapture API development.

Servers for Hackers[18] – Your API has to go somewhere, and unless you're literally made of money, and have some way to get that money through Heroku's payment gateway, then you need to know how to manage a server.

Vagrant Cookbook[19] – Learn how to create effective Vagrant development environments. This book will cover from basic to advanced concepts on Vagrant, including important ProTips to improve your Vagrant projects and avoid common mistakes. The book was updated to cover the new features on Vagrant 1.5, which are substantial compared to previous versions.

---

[17] https://leanpub.com/scalingphp
[18] https://serversforhackers.com/
[19] https://leanpub.com/vagrantcookbook

Made in the USA
Middletown, DE
28 February 2019